I0202214

GOLDEN JUBILEE CONVENTION

SAN FRANCISCO

1931

OFFICIAL REPORT

OF THE

THIRTY - THIRD INTERNATIONAL

CHRISTIAN ENDEAVOR CONVENTION

HELD IN

SAN FRANCISCO, CALIFORNIA

JULY 11-16, 1931.

First Fruits Press
Wilmore, Kentucky
c2015

First Fruits Press

The Academic Open Press of Asbury Theological Seminary

204 N. Lexington Ave., Wilmore, KY 40390

859-858-2236

first.fruits@asburyseminary.edu

asbury.to/firstfruits

ILLUSTRATIONS

GOLDEN
JUBILEE CONVENTION
SAN FRANCISCO
1931

Official Report
of the
Thirty-Third International
Christian Endeavor
Convention

Held in San Francisco, California

July 11-16, 1931

The International Society of Christian Endeavor
Boston, Massachusetts

COPYRIGHT, 1931, BY THE INTERNATIONAL SOCIETY
OF CHRISTIAN ENDEAVOR

Printed in the United States of America

4

CONTENTS

FOREWORD

A Summary of the Golden Jubilee Convention by the President of the International Society of Christian Endeavor

Born in the mind of God, with motive vast, exalted,
And vision vaster than its far-eyed prophet knew,
This plant of Heaven's love and spirit's tending
In brave New England soil took root and grew.

These were the words of my very humble tribute of a decade ago. They are suggestive of my emotion now as I remember the Fiftieth Anniversary Convention of the International Society of Christian Endeavor.

There have been larger conventions than San Francisco 1931. Boston 1893 still claims the record, though modern registration requirements were not then in force. But in my opinion no convention of our movement has ever produced a more comprehensive and convincing program, set more challenging goals, or left so profound an impression upon those who attended it and upon the whole country as this Golden Jubilee gathering at the Golden Gate of the North American Continent.

Fundamental principles and old ideals were reaffirmed and they were given a twentieth century testimony and application. The whole field of the Christian message was surveyed and accepted as youth's opportunity. "For Christ and for the Church" was reaffirmed as our Christian Endeavor motto and "Greater Things Than These" adopted as our immediate and continuing objective.

The two most significant "events" of San Francisco 1931 were: first, the presence of Mother Endeavor Clark; and second, the election of Carlton M. Sherwood to the General Secretaryship.

Christian Endeavor has problems, but they are problems of progress. The past is an inspiration; the future, an invitation; and the present filled with opportunity. "Trusting in the Lord Jesus Christ for strength," we move forward into a great advance—all along the line!

Daniel A. Poling

7

HERBERT HOOVER
President of the United States

PRESIDENT HOOVER'S GREETINGS TO

The International Christian Endeavor Golden Jubilee Convention, San Francisco, Cal., July 16, Broadcast Nation-Wide from Washington and Received in the Convention Auditorium by Ten Thousand Young People

From every State in the United States, from every Province of the Dominion of Canada, from Mexico, and from a score of countries beyond the seas you have assembled in San Francisco to celebrate the golden anniversary of the International Christian Endeavor Society, an organization devoted to golden deeds and ideals.

The fiftieth anniversary of the International Christian Endeavor Society is a notable moment in your history. It is significant not only to you, but to the whole nation by reason of your past services and your potentialities for even greater usefulness in the future.

From a humble beginning in Portland, Me., in 1881, the Christian Endeavor movement has become a world force for the promotion of spiritual advancement among our people. The 4,000,000 members in more than 80,000 local units in 126 nations, dominions, States and island groups present an impressive force in the spiritual well-being of the world.

Despite differences of language, tradition, and custom the youth of the world have found in the organization a common ground for spiritual training and service to their church, community, and country. It represents the most enduring monument to the idealism, insight, and organizing genius of its founder, the late Dr. Francis E. Clark.

The best index to its purposes and values are the principles it stands for. Its loyalties and ideals make for good citizenship, for character and religious faith. It recognizes that national independence and international understanding are not incompatible. It stands for international good will and world peace. It is a mighty force for sobriety, righteousness, and respect for law, patriotism and spiritual development in every nation.

It is an appreciated privilege, in behalf of the nation, to greet the delegates from our land and other lands to the convention of the Christian Endeavor Union at the fiftieth milepost of this dynamic movement.

I congratulate you on the achievements of a half-century of practical idealism. You have before you even higher privileges and opportunities to serve with the vigor, courage, and idealism of youth in the solution of myriads of problems of the future. Above all, yours is a mission of exemplifying the standards of individual conduct which are the basis of national character.

A better world is the mission of youth, and it is your mission.

9

OFFICERS AND COMMITTEES OF THE INTERNATIONAL SOCIETY OF CHRISTIAN ENDEAVOR

DR. DANIEL A. POLING,
President
DR. HOWARD B. GROSE,
Vice-President
DR. WILLIAM HIRAM FOULKES,
Vice-President
CARLTON M. SHERWOOD,
General Secretary
ALVIN J. SHARTLE,
Treasurer and Field Secretary
STANLEY B. VANDERSALL,
Christian Vocations Superintendent
CLARENCE C. HAMILTON,
Publication Manager
ROBERT P. ANDERSON,
Editorial Secretary
DR. IRA LANDRITH,
Citizenship Superintendent
CARROLL M. WRIGHT,
Financial Secretary and Superintendent of Travel and Recreation
DR. PAUL C. BROWN,
Pacific Coast Secretary
HAROLD SINGER,
Mid-West Secretary
W. ROY BREG,
Southern Secretary
STANLEY C. RAMSDEN,
Army and Navy Superintendent
FREDERICK A. WALLIS,
Social Service and Prison Work Superintendent
CHARLES F. EVANS,
Field Representative
CARLTON M. SHERWOOD,
Editor, The Christian Endeavor World
C. C. HAMILTON,
Business Manager, The Christian Endeavor World
STANLEY B. VANDERSALL,
Editor, The Junior Christian Endeavor World
C. C. HAMILTON,
Clerk of the Corporation

Executive Committee

Fred L. Ball
Dr. A. E. Cory
Bert H. Davis
Allan C. Emery
Dr. William Hiram Foulkes
Henry D. Grimes
Mrs. Russell Hewetson
Harry N. Holmes
C. Walter Lotte
Harry E. Paisley

Dr. Daniel A. Poling, *Chairman*
Fred W. Ramsey
Rev. E. L. Reiner
Miss Gertrude L. Stephan
Gene Stone
F. W. Sweney
Wm. J. Von Minden
Hon. Frederick A. Wallis
Prof. Amos R. Wells

Administration Committee

Clarence C. Hamilton
Dr. Daniel A. Poling
Alvin J. Shartle

Carlton M. Sherwood, *Chairman*
Stanley B. Vandersall, *Sec'y*
Carroll M. Wright

Educational Committee

W. Roy Breg
Paul C. Brown
Frank D. Getty
Clarence C. Hamilton
J. Gordon Howard
Cynthia Pearl Maus
Daniel A. Poling
E. W. Praetorius

Alvin J. Shartle
Moses M. Shaw
Carlton M. Sherwood, *Chairman*
Harold Singer
Harry Thomas Stock
Stanley B. Vandersall, *Sec'y*
Carroll M. Wright

THE BOARD OF TRUSTEES

Trustees Representing Evangelical Denominations

Rev. J. Lambert Alexander (Northern Congregational)
Rev. Ernest Bourner Allen, D. D. (Congregational-Christian)
Rev. C. E. Ashcraft, D. D. (United Brethren)
Rev. Albert William Beaven, D. D. (Baptist)
Mr. George W. Coleman (Baptist)
Rev. George M. Diffenderfer (Lutheran)
Mr. James W. Eichelberger (A. M. E. Zion)
Rev. Gilbert Glass, D. D. (Presbyterian U. S., Southern)
Rev. John A. Gregg (United Presbyterian)
Rev. Joseph F. Gross (Evangelical)
Rev. William Ralph Hall, D. D. (Presbyterian, U. S. A.)
Rev. E. E. Harris (United Brethren)
Rev. W. A. Hill. D. D. (Baptist)
Prof. Elmer E. S. Johnson (Schwenkfelder)
Rev. A. B. Kendall, D. D. (Congregational-Christian)

Rev. Henry Churchill King, D. D., LL. D. (Congregational-Christian)
Rev. D. P. Longsdorf (Evangelical Congregational)
Rev. W. A. MacTaggart, D. D. (United Church of Canada)
Rev. Cleland B. McAfee, D. D. (Presbyterian, U. S. A.)
Rev. Arthur Meilicke (Moravian)
Rev. Samuel M. Musselman (Mennonite)
Prof. Clarence E. Pickett (Friends)
Rev. E. M. Riddle (Brethren Church)
Rev. J. B. Showers, D. D. (United Brethren)
Rev. William M. Simpson (Seventh Day Baptist)
Rev. F. H. Snavely (Church of God)
Rev. Floyd W. Tomkins, S T. D. (Episcopal)
Rev. H. T. Unruh (General Conference Mennonites)
Rev. Hugh K. Walker, D. D. (Presbyterian, U. S. A.)
Rev. William L. Washington (Colored Baptist)
Rev. Earle Wilfley, D. D. (Disciples of Christ)

Life Trustees

Rev. Howard B. Grose, D. D.
Mrs. Francis E. Clark
Rev. G. W. Haddaway, D. D.
Rev. P. A. Heilman, D. D.
Mrs. Russell Hewetson

Prof. James Lewis Howe, Ph. D.
Mrs. Daniel A. Poling
Rev. M. Rhodes, D. D.
William Shaw, LL. D.
Mrs. William Shaw

Trustees Representing Denominational Young People's Work

Mrs. James Horace Balm (Reformed in the United States)
Rev. J. M. Bigham (Associate Reformed Presbyterian)
Prof. Aaron Brown (A. M. E. Zion)
David W. Day (Friends)
Rev. Manson Doyle (The United Church of Canada)
Rev. Abram Duryee (Reformed Church in America)
Miss Lucy Eldredge (Congregational-Christian)
Rev. John L. Fairly, D. D. (Presbyterian, U. S.)
Rev. Frank D. Getty (Presbyterian, U. S. A.)
Rev. J. E. Harwood (United Brethren in Christ, Old Constitution)
Rev. J. Gordon Howard (United Brethren)
Rev. W. M. Kannawin (Presbyterian Church in Canada)
Rev. Lawrence C. Little, D. D. (Methodist Protestant)
Miss Cynthia Pearl Maus (Disciples of Christ)
Rev. S. S. Morris, D. D. (African Methodist Episcopal)
Miss Helen Percy (Church of God)
Rev. E. W. Praetorius, D. D. (Evangelical)
Rev. O. P. Schroerluke (Evangelical Synod of North America)
Mr. Moses M. Shaw (United Presbyterian)
Rev. Harry Thomas Stock, D. D. (Congregational-Christian)
Mr. Dan West (Brethren)
Mr. Clark Williamson (Cumberland Presbyterian)

Trustees-at-Large

Rev. Robert P. Anderson
Rev. William M. Anderson, D. D.
Mr. Albert Arend
Mr. Fred L. Ball
Rev. Elmer Becker
Rev. I. W. Bingaman, D. D.
Rev. Bernard C. Clausen, D. D.
Mr. John R. Clements
Rev. F. G. Coffin, D. D.
Mr. Kenneth Colman
Rev. A. E. Cory, D. D.
Rev. O. T. Deever, D. D.
Mr. Allan C. Emery
Mr. Percy S. Foster
Rev. William Hiram Foulkes, D. D.
Mr. O. F. Gilliom
Mr. Henry D. Grimes
Mr. Harry N. Holmes
Mr. Charles H. Jones
Judge Jacob Kanzler
Bishop L. Westinghouse Kyles
Rev. Ira Landrith, D. D., LL. D.
Mr. C. Walter Lotte
Miss Hannah MacBean
Mr. Harry E. Paisley
Mr. Fred D. Parr
Mr. J. C. Penney
Rev. Daniel A. Poling, D. D., LL. D.
Mr. Fred W. Ramsay
Rev. E. L. Reiner
Mr. Thomas Rennie
Mr. Raymond Robins
Mr. C. M. Rodefer
Mr. E. C. Sams
Mr. Paul Shoup
Mr. Virgil A. Sly
Dr. W. C. Smolenski
Rev. George C. Southwell
Miss Gertrude L. Stephan
Rev. H. H. Sweets, D. D.
Mr. F. W. Sweney
Mr. Howard T. Tumilty
Hon. Frederick A. Wallis
Prof. Amos R. Wells, LL. D., Litt. D.
Hon. Curtis D. Wilbur

Trustees Ex Officio

Russell J. Blair
W. Roy Breg
Miss Esther Bremer
Howard L. Brown
Rev. Paul C. Brown, D. D.
Rev. Harold E. Cheyney
Miss Elizabeth Cooper
Alfred C. Crouch
Miss Louella Dyer
Clifford Earle
Rev. Charles F. Evans
Miss Tephia Folsom
Ross Guiley
C. C. Hamilton
George L. Hamlin
Elden Hobbs
Mrs. J. Q. Hook
Warren G. Hoopes
Harold Lovitt
Mrs. Dorothy MacKenzie
Ernest S. Marks
Francis M. Mason
Glen Massman
Frederick L. Mintel
Willard E. Rice
A. J. Shartle
Carlton M. Sherwood
Marion Simms, Jr.
Harold C. Smith
Harold Singer
Rev. Stanley B. Vandersall
Carroll M. Wright

Presidents of State, Provincial and Territorial Unions

Alabama, W. C. Bouldin
Arizona, Miss Verna Harvey
Arkansas, Miss Nettie Kilgore
California, Will H. Vogt
Colorado, Ray F. Smith
Connecticut, Lawrence A. Kipp
Delaware, Miss Emma Huey
District of Columbia, William C. Bond, Jr.
Florida, Clayton C. Crawford
Georgia, L. A. Crow
Idaho, W. Fred Schmid
Illinois, Charles H. Hildebrand
Indiana, Miss Geneva Raum
Iowa, Judge Hubert Utterback
Kansas, Earl K. Duke
Kentucky, Rev. D. N. Roller
Louisiana, Miss Mary Rogillio

Maine, Rev. Harold Nutter
Maryland, H. E. Silverwood
Massachusetts, Clifton P. Howard
Michigan, F. Eldred Pratt
Minnesota, Miss Ethel Boxell
Mississippi, Rev. W. Arnett Gamble
Missouri, Herman F. Vosloh
Montana, Melvin Seitz
Nebraska, Allan K. Longacre
New Hampshire, Percy Q. Morse
New Jersey, Wright E. Thompson
New Mexico, Prof. Walter P. Heinzmann
New York, Harry N. Holmes
North Carolina, Rev. H. C. Kellermeyer
North Dakota, Walter LeRoy
Ohio, Rev. M. D. Kidwell

Oklahoma, Rev. Shelvy Anglemeyer
Oregon, James C. Henderson
Pennsylvania, Earl W. Israel
Rhode Island, Rev. Herbert D. Graetz
South Carolina, Rev. John W. Davis
South Dakota, Miss Nettie C. Turner
Tennessee, E. L. Wuench
Texas, Howard B. Morris
Utah, Miss Lily King
Vermont, Rev. E. Story Hildreth
Virginia, Miss Margaret Richards
Washington, Miss Harriet Leighton
West Virginia, Miss Mary E. Jackson
Wisconsin, Erick L. Madisen
Wyoming, Miss Betty Jenkins
Ontario, Canada, Rev. Fay LeMeadows

Christian Endeavor Field Secretaries

Howard L. Brown, 301 Columbia Bldg., Los Angeles, Calif.
Elden Hobbs, 1127 12th St., Boulder, Colo.
Russell J. Blair, 41 Mt. Vernon St., Boston, Mass.—Conn., R. I.
Mrs. J. Q. Hook, 1012 No. 18th St., Boise, Idaho
Elizabeth Cooper, 2516 No. Alabama St., Indianapolis, Ind.
George L. Hamlin, 619 26th St., Des Moines, Iowa
Francis M. Mason, 712 Kansas Ave., Topeka, Kansas
Rev. Harold E. Cheyney, 516 No. Charles St., Baltimore, Md.
Ernest S. Marks, 14075 Marlowe Ave., Detroit, Mich.
Alfred Crouch, 204 Manufacturers' Exchange Bldg., Kansas City, Mo.
Marion Simms, Jr., St. Edwards, Neb.
Frederick L. Mintel, 6 Woodruff Bldg., Rahway, N. J.
Mrs. Dorothy MacKenzie, W. Surrey Road, Keene, N. H.
Willard E. Rice, 1210 Prudential

Bldg., Buffalo, N. Y.
Esther Bremer, 1023 6th St., So., Fargo, N. D.
Glenn Massman, 1103 United Brethren Bldg., Dayton, Ohio
Tephia Folsom, 314 Empire Bldg., Oklahoma City, Okla.
Ross Guiley, 611 E. 17th Ave., Eugene, Ore.
Warren G. Hoopes, 215 W. Evergreen St., West Grove, Pa.
Harold Lovitt, 608 Construction Bldg., Dallas, Texas
Louella Dyer, 316 Marion Bldg., Seattle, Wash.
Clifford Earle, 5266 37th St., Milwaukee, Wis.
Harold C. Smith, P. O. Box 150, Honolulu, Hawaii
Paul C. Brown, 301 Columbia Bldg., Los Angeles, Calif.
W. Roy Breg, Walton Bldg., Atlanta, Ga.
Charles F. Evans, 1112 Brook St., Louisville, Ky.
Harold Singer, 204 Manufacturers' Exchange Bldg., Kansas City, Mo.

SAN FRANCISCO LOCAL CHRISTIAN ENDEAVOR CONVENTION COMMITTEES

Officers

Paul Shoup, General Chairman
Fred D. Parr, Associate Chairman
Rev. Lloyd R. Carrick, Vice-Chairman
Rev. Herbert P. Shaw, D. D., Vice-Chairman
Rev. Ezra Allen Van Nuys, D. D., Vice-Chairman

Reis Diehl, Secretary
Raymond W. Blosser, Treasurer
Robert D. Moore, Assistant Treasurer
John A. McGregor, Chairman, Finance Committee
William Unmack, Executive Director

The Cabinet

Paul Shoup, Chairman
Fred D. Parr, Associate Chairman
Rev. Lloyd R. Carrick, Rev. Herbert P. Shaw, Rev. Ezra Allen Van Nuys, John A. McGregor, Capt.

Duncan Matheson, Raymond W. Blosser, Harris W. Henderson, Col. Henry G. Mathewson, L. S. Rodgers, William Unmack

Executive

Paul Shoup, General Chairman; Fred D. Parr, Associate Chairman; Reis Diehl, Secretary; William Unmack, Executive Director; Rev. Lloyd R. Carrick, Rev. Herbert P. Shaw, Rev. Ezra Allen Van Nuys, John A. McGregor, Capt. Duncan Matheson, Raymond W. Blosser, Robert D. Moore, Rev. L. I. Chamlee, Rex A Barron, Mrs E. T. Rickman, and the following members "at large": Dr. Daniel A. Poling, Carlton M. Sherwood, Paul C. Brown, Ralph Rambo, Howard Brown, H. Lewis Mathewson, Rev. Luther E. Stein, Rev. Lapsley A. McFee, D. D.

Finance

John A. McGregor, Chairman; Capt. Duncan Matheson, Vice-Chairman; Fred D. Parr, Raymond Blosser, Rev. Herbert P. Shaw, Robert D. Moore, William Unmack

Automobile

L. S. Rodgers, Chairman; Paul Combes, Will Rodgers, Richard H. Thiele, Maynard Morris

Badges

Norman L. MacKinnon, Chairman

Banquets

Earl E. LeFebvre, Chairman; Marian E. Wilson, Secretary; Russell Angel, Treasurer; Ruppert Hutchinson, Financial Secretary; Elmer Rolland Jones, Lois Fenton, Phyllis R. Beal, Nannie J. Foster, J. I. Cochran, Carol Anderson, Agnes Foster, Dorothy Peterson, Peter Barnick, Janie Gibson, Ruth Brown, Tom Murray, Mrs. T. Murray, Mrs. Rustad

Chinatown Trips

Chingwah Lee, Chairman; Mrs. Andrew Wu, Rosemary Lee, L. David Lee, Richard Wong, Albert Park Li

Assisted by: Presbyterian Chinese Junior C. E. Society, Chinese Boy Scouts, Boys and Girls of the Chinese Y. M. C. A. and Y. W. C. A., Students, University of California Chinese Students' Club

Decorations

Mrs. M. S. Harris, Chairman; Marion Day, Amy Barns, Janie Gibson, William Rice, Stanley Taylor, Earl LeFebvre, Ernest C. Karr

Exhibits

Fred R. Roy, Chairman; Eudora Sylvester, Ben March, Mrs. Ray McAfee, Reis Diehl, Harris W. Henderson

First Aid

Dr. Laura B. Hurd, Chairman; Clara Affolter, Winnifred Baurbauer, L. S. Baurbauer, Daniel Crockett, August DeMont, Malcolm Sargent, Edna Speer, Dr. Louise Steel-Brook

Information

Eudora Sylvester, Chairman; Victor Tibbs, Assistant; David Brody, Assistant; Malcolm Sargent, Assistant; Raymond Chong, Harry Pierce, Anna Stewart, Tsune Baba, Catherine Baringer, Neils Andus, Uta Ogawa, Pearl Oliver, Edwin Moore, Esther Jung, Bernice Bryan, Katherine Wall, Donald Ostrander, Wilma Ostrander, Aya Zaiman, Jackson McElvine, Geraldine Beck, Eddie Jung, Charles Walker, Jean Thomson, Miura Kaori, Mary Nelson, Evelyn Barber, Robert Lucero

Intermediate

Benjamin A. March, Chairman; Louise Wall, Secretary; S. Marian Gragham, Mrs. M. R. Izuno, G. A. Culbert, Agnes Robb, Helen Gillette, Mrs. S. Storms, Mrs. Gladys Kohon, Margaret Vail, Ruth March, Mrs. Andrew Y. Een, Mrs. Cameron Brown, Mr. Coats, Gladys Pierce

Junior

Mrs. Ray McAfee, Chairman; Florence Fisher, Secretary; Margaret Verkuyl, Gladys Pierce, Ella Ward, Ruth Cruse, Mrs. C. H. Pool, Charles H. Pool, Jr., Mrs. Law-rence Friedline, Dr. Paul Arnold Peterson, Mrs. Paul Arnold Peterson, Mrs. Edouart Bryant, Mary Maclachlan, Jean Balfour, Mrs. L. F. Rodgers

Halls

Frank I. Turner, Chairman

Hotels

Harry R. Smith, Chairman; Lewis Mathewson, Vice-Chairman; J. E. White, J. Mortimer Culverwell, A. R. Burch, Howard Chinell, Fred Beck, Victory Tibbs, Dwight O. Johnson, Neil C. Fisch, J. B. Hubbard, G. H. Mudd, E. D. Blakely, James C. Randolph, A. S. Anderson, Clarence A. Linn, Harry C. Allen

Mailing

Una L. McGean, Chairman

Pages and Guides

Grace Fors, Chairman; William Thompson Fisher, Vice-Chairman; Ruth McKay, Secretary; Mildred Findlay, Treasurer; William Fisher, Boys' Uniforms; Ramona Martindell, Girls' Uniforms; Walter Headley and Philip Vail, Parade Arrangements: Morma Soderquist, Sign for Parade; Edward Bohmen, Drums; Charles Stringer and Dorothy Fidian, Songs and Yells; Paul Chamlee, Maps; Carola Beetz, Social

Music

Maud E. Dunn, Chairman; Ray McAfee, Assistant Chairman; Harold Cross, Jacob Wiens, Reid Cochran, Mr. and Mrs. A. C. King, G. Vidler, Otto Groeneveld, C. H. Van Marter, Mary E. Stoetzel, Velma O Noll, Mary Ferrell

Official Convention Organist

Rev. Lawrance J. Mitchell

Official Convention Accompanists

Dorothy Rustad, Evalean Hebrard, Bertha Palmer, Mary Brown

Parade

Col. Henry G. Mathewson, Chairman; W. A. Frazier, William Rodgers

Personnel

Rev. L. I. Chamlee, Chairman; Robert Moore, Secretary; Rev. L. R. Carrick, Dr. W. O. Fisher, Earl LeFebvre, Rolland Kirkpatrick, Reis Diehl, Ray McAfee

Program

Rev. Charles L. Duncan, Chairman; Dr. Lloyd R. Carrick, Lewis Mathewson

Publicity

Rex A. Barron, Chairman; Rev. Rudolph Ericson, Lloyd E. Wilson

Pulpit Supply

Rev. James S. West, Chairman

Reception

George F. McLean, Chairman; J. M. Culverwell, Vice-Chairman; Alice M. Cotton, Secretary; Bernard B. Blakeley, Mrs. Bernard B. Blakeley, John R. Titsworth, Flora Hubbard, Edgar H. Owen, Mrs. George F. McLean, David Brodie, Eleanor Hunter, Guy W. Campbell, Una McBean, Tsuni Baba

Poster

Harris W. Henderson, Chairman; H. Lewis Mathewson, Thelma Parsons

Registration

Mrs. E. T. Rickman, Chairman; Grace Fors, Earl LeFebvre, Robert Lundy, Harris W. Henderson, H. Lewis Mathewson, John Ball, C. J. Thomas, C. J. Ellicker, James Otter, Keith Munro

Supplies

Una McBean, Chairman; Jean Christensen, Helen Graham, Marjorie McLeod

Ushering

Frank L. Muncy, Chairman; Norman McKinnon, Assistant Chairman; George A. Gielow, Assistant Chairman; Raymond McDonald, Laurence Freedline, Wilbur McDonald, Nick Chesnes, Allen Van Nuys, Verne Baker, Russell Angel, Lyle Burford, Ray DeVine, Earl Martin, George Wolfenden, Robert Hicks, Robert Wolfenden, Bill Petty, Ernest Peterson, Dick McBean, Lee Davenport, Edward Pierce, Harry Pierce, Edwin Newall, Jim Cochrane, Fred Bostram, W. G. Spencer, Walter Miles, Harold Wright, Alvin Fors, Jack Peterson, Keith Munro, Robert Hill, Orval Morris, Harry Krytzer, Jr., George K. Bowen

"GREATER THINGS THAN THESE"

A Forward Program for Christian Endeavor—Adopted and
Released by the Golden Jubilee Convention, San Fran-
cisco, California, 1931—Goals to Be Reached by
Christian Endeavor Societies and Unions and
Other Groups of Christian Young People

Christian Endeavor's Golden Jubilee is not only a retrospect.
It is a forward look, a FORWARD MARCH—to the realization of more glorious attainments than the past has known, in
the name and for the sake of Christ and the church. A host
of Christian young people send forth these goals that others
may share their accomplishment.

I. A Million Other Young People for Christ

The first step—*Personal Service.*
At least half the members of Christian Endeavor societies enrolled to win their companions for Christ; study-classes and
personal workers' groups organized in every society. (Text-
book suggested, "Acquainting Youth with Christ." International Society of Christian Endeavor, 41 Mt. Vernon St.,
Boston, Mass., 50 cents.)

The second step—*Studying the Life and Teachings of Jesus.*
At least half the members of Christian Endeavor societies en-
gaged in reading and studying anew the Gospel story of
Jesus' life, to inspire those newly committed to Christ, and to
interpret afresh for all Christians the principles of Christ for
themselves and for individual, social, and world relations.
(A new text-book, "The Life of Jesus," a harmony of the
Gospels, is recommended. International Society of Christian
Endeavor, 41 Mt. Vernon St., Boston, Mass., 50 cents.)

The third step—*Cultivating the Devotional Life.*
A fifty-per-cent increase in Comrades of the Quiet Hour
(those who promise to devote at least fifteen minutes every
day to Bible-study, meditation, and prayer).

II. Far-reaching Loyalties for Young People

To Christ—His word, His will, His spirit to be supreme.

To the Church—Increased devotion to the interests of the local church and denomination, including attendance at church services, co-operation with other organizations, participation in denominational enterprises, etc.

To Missions—Fifty-per-cent increase in number of mission-study classes. Fifty-per-cent increase in gifts to mission work.

To Stewardship—Fifty-per-cent increase in number of members of the Tenth Legion. (Those who promise to devote at least one-tenth of their income to Christian work.)

To Christian Endeavor—Fifty-per-cent increase in the number of Christian Endeavor societies. (By grading the societies, by organizing in neighboring churches, etc.)

To Christian Unity—Special attention given to co-operative enterprises which bring together the denominations, and promote a spiritual unity among Christ's followers.

III. Practical Steps in Christian Citizenship

Personal Commitment—Enrolment of all present and former members of Christian Endeavor societies, together with other persons, for personal sobriety, law-observance, and support of the Eighteenth Amendment. (Leaflets suggested: "Then Came Prohibition," 25 cents, and "Will Youth Observe the Law?" 10 cents. International Society of Christian Endeavor. 41 Mt. Vernon St., Boston, Mass.)

Connection with Allied Youth—All members, societies, and unions taking an active part in the program of *Allied Youth* for support of the Eighteenth Amendment and for Christian citizenship.

General Activities—Enlistment of personal, society, and union support of measures looking to the physical, moral, or social welfare of young people.

IV. Advancing Steps toward World Peace

Disarmament—Active co-operation in the circulation of petitions urging the representatives of the United States of America and the Dominion of Canada to use their vote and influence in the World Disarmament Conference, February, 1932, in favor of further disarmament among the nations.

Agitation—Increased promotion of study-classes, essay contests, debates, discussion courses, etc., on the subject of international co-operation and the outlawry of war, to the end of establishing the will toward peace and friendship throughout the world.

The Late Dr. Francis E. Clark and "Mother" Clark
who founded our organization fifty years ago

CHAPTER I

BEFORE THE CONVENTION

Friday, July 10, and Saturday, July 11
Youth Gathers at the Golden Gate—A Feast of
Inspiration—The Reports of the Officers

JULY 10 and 11 have been days of special trains and special cars in the railroad terminals of San Francisco, windy and sunlit metropolis of the Pacific. The Golden Jubilee Presidential Special, in charge of Carroll M. Wright, travel and recreation superintendent of the International Society of Christian Endeavor, reached the convention city at 9.30 o'clock Saturday morning. On board were Mrs. Francis E. Clark, Mrs. Daniel A. Poling, W. Roy Breg, Southern secretary of the International Society, Warren G. Hoopes, field secretary of the Pennsylvania Christian Endeavor Union, and about two hundred Endeavorers from fifteen States.

A few minutes before, several hundred members from the Los Angeles County Christian Endeavor Union had arrived in charge of California's field secretary, Howard L. Brown.

Other special tour parties, traveling by railroad, included the following:

New England. In charge of Russell J. Blair, Boston.
Ohio and Michigan. In charge of Rev. Herman A. Klahr, Cleveland, and Ernest S. Marks, Detroit.
New York and New Jersey. In charge of Fred L. Mintel, Rahway, N. J., and Willard E. Rice, Buffalo.
Indiana. In charge of Miss Elizabeth Cooper, Indianapolis.
Wisconsin. In charge of Clifford Earle, Milwaukee.
Missouri. In charge of Alfred C. Crouch, Kansas City, Mo.
Nebraska.

A special car left the Texas Christian Endeavor Convention at El Paso on July 6, and brought an enthusiastic delegation.

Colorado, Missouri, Oregon, and Kansas were among the States sending particularly large delegations by automobile. As the delegates arrive at the more than thirty hotels in which their registrations for the convention period have been made, license plates from every State of the Union may be seen. The automobiles, decorated and filled with young people, have attracted much attention in downtown San Francisco.

With the Presidential Special

President Poling traveled with the Golden Jubilee special train via Pennsylvania and Santa Fé from New York to Winslow, Ariz. Here, with Carlton M. Sherwood, extension secretary and editor of THE CHRISTIAN ENDEAVOR WORLD, he left by airplane for Los Angeles to fill an important engagement. Clarence C. Hamilton, publication manager, and Alvin J. Shartle, treasurer of the International Society, were members of the Golden Jubilee tour party as it crossed several Western States.

HONORING THE PIONEER MOTHERS

Proctor's wonderful group on a high hill at Kansas City, Mo., honors the women of the Western plains who pushed forward with their families to claim new lands. How fitting that Mrs. Francis E. Clark, mother of Christian Endeavor, should pause before this bronze memorial!

At Chicago, before boarding the cars in the Santa Fé station, Mr. Wright and his party gathered for a fellowship dinner in the Hotel Stevens, Chicago.

On the following morning, at Kansas City, Mo., the delegates left their cars to participate on invitation in the worship of the Independence Boulevard Christian Church. The pastor, Rev. Raphael H. Miller, introduced Dr. Poling and Mother Clark, both of whom spoke in the morning church service following an impressive observance of the Lord's Supper. Carlton M. Sherwood spoke to four hundred men in the Sunday-school session.

On Monday the entire party was taken up Pike's Peak, from Colorado Springs, in large open cars over a thirty-mile automobile highway. A clear and almost cloudless vista from the peak greeted the Endeavorers.

A full day was spent at Grand Canyon. A three-hour automobile trip to the Petrified Forest was another treat of the tour. A lunch at Mission Inn, Riverside, Cal., one of the most interesting hotels in the world, preceded the coming of the Christian Endeavor party to Los Angeles, where one night and a full day were spent. Some members left the party here for a side-trip to Yosemite National Park. The other members entrained July 10 for San Francisco, and arrived on time, to be met by a large representation from the reception committee.

Kansas City Endeavorers extended splendid hospitality during the visit of a number of hours to this city that had entertained the 1929 International Convention. Charles D. Williams, who was general chairman for the 1929 local committee, was among the leaders who greeted the visitors. At San Bernardino, Cal., a number of Christian Endeavorers served lemonade to the thirsty travelers and a crate of oranges was put on board. Los Angeles Endeavorers personally greeted all members of the Golden Jubilee and other tour parties, and flowers and a letter of greeting were given to each one.

A Feast of Inspiration

The convening of the delegates in the first mass-meeting was still some hours distant—but the preliminary sessions were significant beyond all precedent.

Even before the convention day a noteworthy preparatory banquet of fellowship and inspiration was held. This had been planned as a local meeting of the San Francisco Convention committee and friends of the Bay Cities, to honor speakers and officers. In spirit, it proved to be the great opening session of the Golden Jubilee Convention.

Nearly five hundred enthusiastic supporters of the convention gathered Friday evening, July 10, in the Bellevue Hotel under the scintillating toast-mastership of Paul Shoup, general chairman of the convention, and president of the Southern Pacific Lines, with the assistance of Fred D. Parr, co-chairman of the local committee.

What a meeting it was! Mr. Parr called for the reports of the many committee chairmen. All indicated that plans had been completed at least a week before the convention opened, and every chairman in turn testified to the joy he or she had in the preparations for this event.

Said Mr. Parr: "We have made no sacrifice. It has rather been a pleasure and an inspiration to plan for this great gathering."

City Contributed Funds

City Treasurer Matheson, an ardent Christian Endeavorer, told of the financial support provided by the municipality from the public treasury. Mr. Shoup in his inimitable way introduced the various International Society officers and convention speakers.

Carlton M. Sherwood, extension secretary of the International Society, paid a tribute to the local committee, in which he said that the speakers had agreed that, individually and collectively, the San Francisco leadership represented men and women of as fine a spirit and as high a caliber as have ever served on a convention committee.

The treasurer of the International Society, Alvin J. Shartle, paid a tribute to the committee's work, as did Stanley B. Vandersall, Christian-vocations superintendent, Clarence C. Hamilton, publication-manager. Harold Singer, mid-West secretary, and Paul C. Brown, Pacific-Coast secretary.

What speeches were made—short, but scintillating! Colonel Raymond Robins, social economist and philanthropist, thrilled the audience with his own testimony as to the need of the hour and the place of Christian Endeavor in filling that need.

Dr. J. Whitcomb Brougher kept the audience in an uproar of laughter with his humor and searching comments. Dr. William Hiram Foulkes, of Newark, N. J., chairman of the program committee, reminded the diners of the spiritual power of the convention in the lives of young people.

Dr. Herbert P. Shaw, pastor of the West Side Christian Church, voiced the welcome of the San Francisco pastors.

Harry N. Holmes, president of the New York State Christian Endeavor Union, captured the audience as he called for youth's loyalty to "unchanging ideals in a changing world."

Dr. Poling never spoke with greater eloquence than in his pre-convention address at this banquet.

Six members of the 1897 San Francisco Convention committee were present, and were greeted with a rousing cheer.

With a prayer and a song the pre-convention banquet closed. sending its members away with emotions touched and great expectations for the convention days ahead.

In All Things—Prayer

A pre-convention prayer meeting was held Saturday afternoon, July 11, in the beautiful Methodist Episcopal Church next door to the headquarters hotel. This is one of the finest churches in San Francisco, cathedral-like in its dimensions, and arched above like the churches of the Middle Ages.

The leader of the meeting was A. J. Shartle, treasurer of the International Society, and the speakers were Homer Rodeheaver, superb song leader, and Bishop L. Westinghouse Kyles, of the A. M. E. Zion Church. Mr. Rodeheaver told of the place and purpose of music in life and worship, and of how, like an infection, it spreads from heart to heart. Even thus early, this promised to be a singing convention, a promise that was amply fulfilled in later sessions. Bishop Kyles followed with an able address, evangelical in content, helpful, uplifting and inspiring.

The Trustees Meet

The first meeting of the trustees took place in the William Taylor Hotel on Friday morning with Dr. Poling in the chair.

First of all, Dr. Poling introduced the First Lady in Christian Endeavor, Mrs. Francis E. Clark herself, who had come all 'the way from Boston to attend the meetings. Greetings were brought from several who were prevented by illness from attending the convention: Dr. William Shaw, former general secretary of Christian Endeavor, Dr. Howard B. Grose, who long ago gave to Christian Endeavorers the Christian Endeavor monogram, and Percy S. Foster, magnificent song leader, who has served in many conventions in days gone by. Illness in the family prevented Dr. Ira Landrith from being present.

Work is progressing in having made a memorial stained-glass window for Williston Congregational Church, Portland, Me., where the first Christian Endeavor society was formed. The window is made possible largely through the generosity of Mrs. Francis E. Clark.

The Christian Endeavor Advisory Committee for work in the South was continued, a fine tribute being paid to excellent work done by its members.

Officers' Reports

A. J. Shartle, treasurer and field secretary of the International Society, led off in presenting reports from officers. He told of long journeys and visits to many States in the interest of Christian Endeavorers, and of the splendid condition in which he found the movement in all his travels.

Rev. Robert P. Anderson, editorial secretary, described his work, covering the writing of a "Life of Jesus," "The Daily Companion," "The Intermediate Companion," a booklet entitled "Christian Endeavor in Every Land," and so forth.

The report of C. C. Hamilton, publication manager, showed a very satisfactory condition in spite of the current business depression, which has affected trade of all kinds. He told of various new publications, "The Life of Jesus," "Leadership through Christian Endeavor," "A Son's Portrait of His Father," being a biography of Dr. Clark, and especially a "New Hymnal for Christian Youth." His further report as publication manager of THE CHRISTIAN ENDEAVOR WORLD showed some of the difficulties under which this magazine is laboring. He urged all to help secure subscriptions and thus place the paper on a paying basis.

Stanley B. Vandersall reported as Christian vocations secretary. He told of an immense amount of work done in meetings, on college campuses, and through literature, describing the various services rendered by his department. Besides this he has taken over the editorship of THE JUNIOR CHRISTIAN ENDEAVOR WORLD, and some of the duties of the general secretary.

Carroll M. Wright reported having taken on the work of financial secretary in addition to his work as manager of the travel department. He reported that the Christian Endeavor party of 190, brought from the East to the convention, is the largest party of any kind brought from East to West this year to any gathering. But for the depression this number would have been greatly increased.

Charles F. Evans, who has been Western representative of the International Society, with headquarters in Chicago, became CHRISTIAN ENDEAVOR WORLD field representative when it was decided some months ago to close the Chicago office. He told of his campaign and of the work he had been able to do for Christian Endeavor while on the road.

The report of Carlton M. Sherwood, extension secretary, was a record of a prodigious amount of work well done. Besides his work as extension secretary he took on at the New Year responsibility for the program and promotion of this convention, and the editorship of THE CHRISTIAN ENDEAVOR WORLD. In addition to this he has served as executive secretary of the Citizens' Committee of One Thousand for Law Observance.

Southern secretary, W. Roy Breg, told of a year of high achievement in Dixie. He spent 232 days in the field, attended innumerable gatherings, and closed the year with a gain of 361 new societies organized, or more than an average of one a day for twelve months.

Dr. Paul C. Brown, Pacific Coast secretary, does field work in California, Montana, Idaho, Utah, Oregon and Washington. In California more than 400 societies were organized in the past year and the net gain in membership amounts to 7,000. According to this report, which was full of good cheer, the work in California is progressing and is stronger today than ever.

Harold Singer is secretary for the Mid-West. In the past year he has travelled more than 75,000 miles in his vast parish. In every one of these Mid-West States the number of societies has increased, and the attendance of pastors at conferences and conventions has also increased.

The trustees, rejoicing in these reports, felt again the sources of strength inherent in this Christian youth movement, and realized anew the scope of the work carried forward.

This first day may well be called ''The Day of the Forward Look.''

THE VANGUARD OF HAWAII'S DELEGATES

The Mid-Pacific Union was represented at San Francisco by forty Christian Endeavorers. Each wore the leis of Hawaiian tradition, and these bright-colored trophies were presented to several of the International Society officers.

REV. DANIEL A. POLING, D.D., LL.D., S.T.D.
*President, International Society of Christian Endeavor
and of the World's Christian Endeavor Union*

CHAPTER II

"GREATER THINGS THAN THESE"

Saturday Evening, July 11
Ten Thousand Gather for the Keynote Session—Past Blessings Are Recalled and a New Program Is Launched under the Leadership of President Poling

IN a spirit of reverent joy, thousands of Christian Endeavorers in the beautiful Exposition Auditorium in San Francisco began on Saturday evening, July 11, the convention that celebrates the movement's fiftieth birthday. On five succeeding evenings, youth, would swarm into this great hall—one of the largest and finest in the country. But to every convention-goer, this first keynote session—smaller in numbers than the great crowd of Sunday night—will be a matchless memory.

"Greater Things than These" was the theme of this opening session—a review of the blessings and triumphs of the past half-century and a call into action that lies ahead. President Daniel A. Poling was never more powerful as preacher and prophet, commanding youth's life in his Master's service, than in the key-note address of this session. Those who were present will never forget this message—emotional, but founded on fine and logical thinking; idealistic, yet with an intensely practical foundation.

"Greater Things than These" becomes a phrase to win back precious memories for all who were in the San Francisco Convention on its opening night.

Ushered in by Song

Homer Rodeheaver and the all-California chorus of 500 voices sang before the meeting was convened, and conducted a music festival following the benediction. The auditorium is well suited to music. An organ played by Rev. Lawrance J. Mitchell and two pianos accompany the chorus.

The pianists who serve in rotation in the convention sessions are Misses Dorothy Rustad, Evalean Hebrard, Bertha

27

Palmer, and Mary Brown. The "New Hymnal for Christian Youth," in blue binding decorated with gold for the Jubilee Year, is the convention's song book.

Dr. Herbert P. Shaw, of West Side Christian Church, San Francisco, gave the invocation.

Both General Chairman Paul Shoup and Associate Chairman Fred D. Parr represented the convention committee in extending the welcome of San Francisco and California churches and Endeavorers. Mr. Shoup, president of the Southern Pacific Lines, spoke of the 1897 International Convention at San Francisco, which had profoundly affected the Christian life of the city. "San Francisco has aspirations to become a beacon light in art, education, culture, and things of the spirit. It is here that Orient and Occident meet and we would be a centre for all that is best in modern life," he said. Mr. Shoup added, "I feel that Christian Endeavor has a broader power for good than possibly any other church organization."

"Whatever He Would Have Me Do"

Captain Duncan Matheson for the city, and Colonel Carlos Huntington for the State, cordially welcomed the delegates. "California Exults" was one interpretation Colonel Huntington gave to the initials C E. Harry N. Holmes, for W. N. Jenkins of Oakland, presented a rosewood gavel, trimmed with gold, to President Poling.

A high moment in the historic session came. Mrs. Francis E. Clark was introduced and greeted with an ovation. "My friends at home thought I was too old to come away out here for the convention," she said, in her clear, almost youthful voice. "But fifty years ago I told my Saviour that, trusting in His strength, I would strive to do whatever He would like to have me do. The only question I had to settle was whether or not Jesus wanted me to come to San Francisco. I thought I would give Him the benefit of the doubt. Mr. Clark had hoped he could be here for the Golden Jubilee, but he was called to higher service. Trusting in Jesus for strength, I have come hoping that I might perhaps say something here that would cause young people to be helpful and loyal to Christ and to the Church, and to stand always for the things that have been associated with Christian Endeavor."

Five members of the San Francisco Convention committee of 1897 were introduced, and James F. Webster, associate chairman of the committee, brought the greetings of these veteran Endeavorers.

And now the event of the evening—the president's keynote address. The full text follows.

GREATER THINGS THAN THESE
A Message to the Youth of North America
By Dr. Daniel A. Poling

The San Francisco International Christian Endeavor Convention celebrates the Golden Anniversary of what is perhaps the greatest youth movement in the world.

On February 2, 1881, in the parsonage of Williston Church, Portland, Maine, Francis E. Clark and his wife, Harriet Abbott Clark, who honors this Convention with her presence and will bless it with her personality, organized the first Christian Endeavor society.

The boys and the girls who gathered in the home of their minister that afternoon came with the spirit of a successful revival meeting that had just closed. In that spirit this movement was born. With it Christian Endeavor has gone forward into all the earth.

Francis E. Clark was one of the greatest of Christian statesmen, distinguished in personal character and in public achievement, scholarly, sacrificial, and with unsurpassed genius for organizing a great ideal. His faith was simple and ceaseless and became triumphant. He is remembered and loved as the "good St. Francis of the world's youth."

Beginning in January of this year, continuing through the spring and moving forward now into the summer, in 126 nations, states, dominions, or island groups, anniversary meetings have been held. Representatives of more than 80,000 individual societies, in nearly a hundred evangelical communions, have come together with reverence for the memory of the great man who became "Father Endeavor Clark", and with gratitude to God for achievements recorded and yet greater opportunities on ahead.

To Climax the Spirit of Berlin, 1930

In one sense this convention is the echo meeting of "Berlin, 1930", the Eighth World's Christian Endeavor Convention. But, in a sense even more significant, it may become the climax of that memorable gathering. We convene in the spirit of Berlin's closing session and shall move forward with the eagerness of its marching song, "The Path of Peace Proclaim." We shall strive to realize here the prophecy of that never-to-forgotten night when the flags of forty-two nations changed hands, when Europe's largest auditorium became a pulsing purpose for Christian unity, and when an open door of life and service was set before our streaming eyes.

We rejoice in the presence tonight of those other associates of Francis E. Clark,—Dr. Howard Grose, Vice-President of the International Society of Christian Endeavor, and of Dr. William Shaw, "Field Marshal" and "Executive Prime Minister" of our movement over a longer period than any other man has ever served.

Dr. Grose designed the Christian Endeavor badge. William Shaw, next to Francis E. Clark, made it what it has become—the supreme emblem of Christian youth. He more than any other man is responsible for my continuing life in Christian Endeavor.

We think of others tonight—Amos R. Wells, Christian Endeavor editor and man of letters without a peer; Samuel W. Adriance, our second general secretary; George Coleman; Hiram Lathrop; and George B. Graff; ah, and of that immortal trio that with Francis E. Clark look down upon us from the battlements of heaven—John Willis Baer, James Hill, and Dr. George M. Ward. These three were called to their immortal triumph during the past year.

Officers, International Society of Christian Endeavor

WM. HIRAM FOULKES,
D.D., LL.D.,
Vice-President

HOWARD B. GROSE, D.D.
Vice-President

DANIEL A. POLING
D.D., LL.D., S.T.D.,
President

FREDERICK A. WALLIS
*Social Service and
Prison Work Supt.*

HAROLD SINGER
Mid-West Secretary

IRA LANDRITH,
D.D., LL.D.,
Citizenship Supt.

ROBERT P. ANDERSON
Editorial Secretary

S. C. RAMSDEN
*Army and Navy
Superintendent*

30

CARROLL M. WRIGHT
*Travel and Recreation
Superintendent
Financial Secretary*

CARLTON M. SHERWOOD
General Secretary

S. B. VANDERSALL
*Christian Vocations
Superintendent*

ALVIN J. SHARTLE
*Treasurer and Field-
Secretary*

CHARLES F. EVANS
Field Representative

PAUL C. BROWN
Pacific Coast Secretary

C. C. HAMILTON
Publication Manager

W. ROY BREG
Southern Secretary

The Statistics of Our Progress

The reports of our Secretaries and of the Administration Committee will bring us the records of the past biennium and the summary of five decades. The program of this convention will unfold the details of our departments and committees—Junior and Intermediate, Missionary, Quiet Hour, Prayer Meeting, Tenth Legion and Citizenship, Alumni and Lookout, Rural Christian Endeavor, Floating Christian Endeavor, Prison Christian Endeavor, Christian Endeavor among the lepers, and all the rest. Evangelism, vocational guidance, and the story of the Life-Work Recruits are all at the heart of our missionary enterprise. Christian Endeavor Extension is the rallying call of a hundred languages and dialects.

My report at the recent World's Convention listed societies as follows. There have been no tabulations of increases since that time, but these increases have been considerable, with a national movement added in Italy.

Continents	Countries	Societies
Central America . . .	4	25
South America . .	10	176
Europe . .	28	12,938
Africa	8 groups or countries	756
Australasia . . .	2 dominions	2,523
Asia	12 countries or divisions	6,088
Islands . . .	33 islands or groups	551
North America . . .	8 countries or divisions	57,056

Total number of countries, dominions, divisions, groups or islands, 105.
Total number of societies, 80,113.

But again we must remind ourselves that our strength is not in numbers, and that the only justification for looking backward is that we may glory in the Cross and press on with yet greater eagerness and higher faith toward the mark of our high calling in Jesus Christ. In this convention we shall rededicate ourselves to these principles that are basic in our movement and to the evangelical reality that has made us what we are.

Christian Endeavor is not a youth club. It is a Christian society of young people. And as the C surrounds the E in the pin we wear, Christ Himself must surround our movement; our whole enterprise and all our endeavors must center in Him.

Significantly we both stand fast and go forward. "San Francisco, 1931", shall under God lead the young people of the North American continent through the door opened in "Berlin, 1930." To be worthy of our inheritance, to express in any adequate fashion our appreciation for what others have done and for what we have entered into, we must find in these days a new determination and a fresh passion for service.

From the Christian Endeavorers of New Zealand comes a worthy motto for youth's advance into the next fifty years, fifty years of Endeavor to Christianize the whole of life—"Greater Things than These!"

As an organization the Christian Endeavor movement is not apart from but within the church. "For Christ and the Church" is more than a motto; it is a definition of the very genius of our Society. Evangelically and evangelistically Christian, Christian Endeavor receives its definition of faith and its theological interpretations from the particular communion in which it moves and has its being. Always Christian Endeavor plans should harmonize with the programs of individual churches and communions.

The interdenominational International Society is not a governing body. We hope that it may more and more become a dynamo for generating enthusiasm, a clearing-house for plans and methods, a platform of fellowship and agreement, an indispensable and strong arm to every youth project within the church, and always a spiritual unity in Christ. That sentence is filled with mixed metaphor, but the possibilities of Christian Endeavor are even more diverse!

Personal Tribute to the Society's Value

I am a competent witness to the unique value of Christian Endeavor in the life of the individual church. I have watched personally its ministry in all types of communities. I have come through its activities and departments. I have been both a Christian Endeavor secretary and a pastor. I could not think of a pastorate anywhere without Christian Endeavor.

I repeat that of all agencies in my ministry it has been the most effective for training young people for Christian service, for promoting Christian fellowship and for relating young people to Christian work at the point of their greatest efficiency. It is one of Christianity's deepest fountains. Specifically it is a society, an organizational personality—not merely a department in Christian education, though it is that, too.

This convention should make a contribution toward the correlation of particular programs, the co-ordinating of all educational work within the church. Such correlation is desirable and imperative. Christian Endeavor desires to serve, and serve with the Sunday school, the church school, the boys' club, the girls' club, and the organized Bible classes.

Again and again, year after year, in thousands and tens of thousands of instances, Christian Endeavor, through evangelism, personal and congregational, has made the evangelistic emphasis and the evangelistic message both possible and powerful.

New Occasions Teach New Duties

Certainly progress is possible. Certainly new achievements are an obligation taught by new occasions.

Your president has recommended to the trustees of the International Society general and specific changes in our constitution and in certain of our official relationships, changes that will, we believe, bring both the opportunities and the responsibilities of the movement even closer to the young people themselves.

Christian Endeavor should continue to be distinctively a movement of the young people.

The recommendations for revisions invite the careful scrutiny of our State, district, county, and city union programs and procedures. The development of our work within the States, counties, and cities has moved more rapidly than the adaptation and enrichment of our methods. Here is a field in which may be developed yet greater efficiency.

Forward March to New Opportunities

We have also recommended to the trustees the inauguration of a campaign to gather a Fiftieth Anniversary Maintenance and Extension Fund. Perhaps no other organization in the world today—certainly no organization of this character and of so large a membership—has gone forward under so conservative a financial program as has Christian Endeavor.

It is our purpose, and a sound purpose, not to depart from this policy. From the organizational standpoint, the chief glory of our Society is volunteer leadership. Year after year, decade after decade, the Christian Endeavor movement has renewed itself locally, nationally, and internationally. Through all its departments the Society has carried on with few salaried workers, but under the leadership of hundreds of thousands of boys and girls, young men and young women, who have been encouraged to learn by doing.

But today great obligations and unparalleled opportunities confront us. In at least nineteen countries there are imperative needs that can only be met on the missionary basis, and with American Christian Endeavor financing the initial activities or subsidizing the heroic local efforts.

The Waldensian Church, the glorious ancient church of Italy, has just come into our fellowship. It brings to us a perfectly marvelous demonstration of faith and sacrifice. Already more than a score of local groups have been established. But the Waldensian Church is both heroic and poor. It has not asked for our charity,—and yet even one hundred dollars means almost the difference between defeat and victory.

Italy is but one example of many harvests that are white. We should locate at the earliest possible môment European headquarters in the city of Geneva. With unanswerable logic and deep emotion our splendid Hungarian Christian Endeavorers pleaded for this when we were with them in their national convention last August. More, they asked that this leadership come from the World's Union. We promised them, as we promised others, that, God helping us and at the earliest possible moment, we would finance such a project.

And South America waits. The World's Sunday School Convention is to be held in Buenos Aires next summer. Our Sunday school associates have invited us to participate. That continent of missionary opportunity is our opportunity too.

To maintain Christian Endeavor at home and abroad, to hold fast this goal and to advance our flag of fellowship and service, to join our comrades in Italy, in the new nations of Europe, in Africa and Asia, Christian Endeavor in her Golden Anniversary year must bring her gifts of treasure as well as of life.

We believe that we shall make "San Francisco, 1931," memorable for this new advance; that we shall launch here one of the greatest. one of the most significant, movements in the history of our organization. We have discussed with the trustees and we propose tonight. "The Fiftieth Anniversary Maintenance and Extension Fund—Two Million Dollars."

Our Golden Anniversary Goals

These goals are all for the two-year period directly ahead.

The proposed program of the International Society of Christian Endeavor, while a particular program, is in complete harmony with the campaign launched at Berlin. Therefore, we continue the Crusade with Christ.

First, we propose the *Crusade with Christ to Win a Million Other Youths.* Again evangelism is first. To this end, we ask that our State, county, district, and city unions adopt definite goals as follows:

A fifty per cent increase in the enrollment of personal workers.

A fifty per cent increase in the membership of study classes in the life of Jesus.

A fifty per cent increase in the membership of Comrades of the Quiet Hour.

Where these activities have been neglected or allowed to lapse, they should be revived with all the urge of a new affection. Let us set up everywhere a definite plan for evangelistic effort. Christian Endeavor was born in a revival. Christian Endeavor thrives best in such an atmosphere. The call to confess sin, to seek forgiveness, to discover the Christ as Saviour and Lord, the call to the changed and dedicated life—the life of devotion to the person and plan, to the will and to the way, of the Galilean—this call is the very life call of Christian Endeavor.

To the individual Christian the joy that is supreme is the joy that comes with the realization of the fact that one has been used in some way, however small in present appearance, but in some way to lead another to Him who is "faithful and just to forgive."

Second, Crusade with Christ "for Christ and the Church." "For Christ and the church." "Greater things than these." Here is the perfect combination of motto and program, of tradition and prophecy, of past and present—the perfect combination of all elements of true power and greatness for future achievement. Let us set up in San Francisco a program in terms of loyalty to the local church, loyalty to the denomination or communion; a program in definite service and in systematic giving for activities of the church at home and abroad. Let this loyalty be characterized by an immediate concentration on the tasks that are right at hand.

Christian Endeavor, in her contribution to the teaching force of the Sunday school and to the leadership personnel of every other department of the parish, has a worthy past. The future should see past results conserved and expanded for even larger results.

We propose a fifty per cent increase in the number of tithers and the acceptance of definite tithing goals in all our unions. Missionary retrenchment that has broken the hearts of our great leaders will be a thing of the past if Christian Endeavor and other like agencies place an adequate emphasis upon systematic giving.

One million tithers in the Protestant Church of North America would solve every missionary problem of this decade.

We propose a fifty per cent increase in the number of mission study classes.

We propose as a goal in Christian Endeavor extension a fifty per cent increase in the number of new societies. This goal is located under the Crusade with Christ, "for Christ and the church", because the Christian Endeavor society *is* within and part of the church and belongs nowhere else.

Crusading for Church Union

Finally, in this second goal "for Christ and the church", let us crusade for church unity. Christian Endeavor has been a demonstration of unity in action, of co-operative enterprise well done, of united ministries at home and abroad. It has brought a better understanding between the young people of many communions, of many races, and of many nations. It has been identified with federated enterprises, and in this field has often helped bring success out of failure. But, beyond anything that has been accomplished thus far within the Protestant Church, the present crisis in religion demands that we achieve *united action*. Our schisms have become indeed a sin, a sin against Christ's redemptive plan for both the individual and the social order.

Certainly we must not make haste at the expense of real progress.

Certainly we must not seek organic union in spite of spiritual division. But just as certainly we must trust faith rather than fear, and obey God rather than man, or lose the war to win the world to Christ.

No one denomination or communion, nor all denominations or communions working separately, however sacrificially, are sufficient for this crisis. If we cannot conquer our own littleness, we can never overcome the enemy's largeness. Christian Endeavor in her Fiftieth Anniversary Convention offers her resources of youth and spirit, offers herself, to help to bring it to pass.

For Building a Civic Conscience

Third, Crusade with Christ for Christian Citizenship. "Render unto Caesar the things that belong to Caesar and unto God the things that belong to God" defines the approach of our movement to the problems of government.

We believe that patriotism begins at home, that we cannot be truly Christian unless we are earnestly striving to be worthy and alert members of the community and state. An aroused civic conscience, registering itself at the polls on election day, is a first requisite for good government. The bootlegger and the racketeer are an indictment not only of the venal and delinquent public official but of indifference in private life. Eternal vigilance is the price of liberty. I commit a crime against society when I fail to pay the price.

This government will not fall because of attack from abroad. It will not succumb to the propaganda of the Soviet. We need not fear from enemies that may embark from distant shores. Dry-rot from within is the only fatal menace.

Poverty has never destroyed a proud people. No bondage imposed upon a nation from without has ever been finally confirmed. The blood of martyrs has been the seed of the church; and the martyrdom of patriots, the ravishing of political units—these have ruined the mightiest conquerors of history. But never yet has any civilization risen superior to internal decadence.

It needs no prophet to declare that unless the United States finds a way to distribute the benefits and the economic security of her national prosperity more widely—unless within her present system she reorganizes industry, makes the average man secure in his savings, renounces personal license, which bears so widely the false name of personal liberty, confirms the sovereignty of law and accepts at fair cost to herself America's mandate to help organize the world against war—this government of which Washington is called the "Father" and Lincoln the "Saviour" will perish from the earth.

Poverty Must Be Destroyed

Prohibition is not the only issue. We are not interested in prohibition to the exclusion of other matters. Political decisions should not be conditioned exclusively upon whether or not parties are dry and candidates are for the Eighteenth Amendment. American Democracy must find a way to destroy poverty. The American social and economic system must accept responsibility for discovering how to give work to every willing worker, for making the average man more secure in his savings and for distributing more widely the higher privileges of life as well as the bare necessities. The passion of the Soviet to win a class war must be matched by the fervor of American Democracy to perfect "this freedom." American youth wait on the call of such a leadership. In delay is the promise of disaster. But youth does not consent to failure. We believe in the future of American Democracy. The United States shall win through. In this faith, Christian Endeavor dedicates herself to youth's tasks of citizenship.

First, for our citizenship goals, let us adapt the spirit of Christian Endeavor to the particular needs and opportunities of our community life.

We propose here that a bill be introduced in the next session of Congress to make illegal the shipment by express and freight of lewd pictures and lewd literature. The post-office and mails are closed to tons of filth that in pictures, magazines, and book form crowd the news-stands today. By freight and by express this pestilential stuff, this sewage, is given an open channel across the continent. To stop this flow, let San Francisco, 1931, recommend such a bill as proposed.

Manifestly our message tonight cannot itemize all the interests with which as Christian Endeavorers we should be identified. The motion-picture, the radio, have greatly complicated the common problem, and Sabbath desecration is as a steadily rising tide.

We would not confine ourselves to denunciations. We would be constructive and positive. We rejoice in many indications of a revival in the common decencies and of a return to the so-called Victorian moralities. But the road ahead is long, and some of us have not yet begun the march.

Twenty years ago,—exactly twenty years ago, at the Atlantic City Convention in 1911,—Ira Landrith and Howard Grose wrote for us the motto that thrilled a nation to attention and that sent millions into action for national prohibition, "A Saloonless Nation by 1920—the three hundredth year from the landing of the Pilgrims at Plymouth."

Called to the Prohibition Colors

Tonight the United States of America faces a greater crisis than that of twenty years ago. We are in a struggle to determine whether or not this plan of government is justified, whether or not constitutional procedure can be maintained, whether or not government by nullification is to be substituted for the Eighteenth Amendment. Upon this determination rests in no small measure the hope, the very destiny, of what we have called American freedom.

Again we do not consent to failure. We launch here a new and greater campaign for the Eighteenth Amendment and for liberty with law. We commend to you all the splendid agencies that are active in this vast and vital field—the Anti-Saloon League, the Woman's Christian Temperance Union, the Intercollegiate Prohibition Association, and the particular boards of temperance in the various communions.

Particularly we would endorse the new and united campaign of the Allied Forces, a campaign that is to sweep across the country with mass meetings, literature distribution, and the organization of local agencies. We hope for this campaign great success. We believe that it may very materially effect the national political conventions of 1932.

But of this great movement, which comprises Allied Business Men, Allied Women, and Allied Youth, it is with Allied Youth that we have a particular opportunity. Allied Youth is a movement for young people and led by young people that capture the youthful imagination. We would call you to its colors. You will be given the opportunity to enlist under its flag, and in your own communities and States we shall count on your support for its progress of education and enrollment.

At the Cleveland International Convention four years ago thousands of delegates stood together, stood in a mighty unanimous verdict of approval, and declared with uplifted hands, "No political party or candidate not declaring for prohibition and for prohibition-enforcement can have our support or vote." In San Francisco let that commitment be reaffirmed. From San Francisco let us move out, as twenty years ago Christian Endeavor moved from Atlantic City—from San Francisco let us move out to give our best and all to what David Lloyd George has called "the greatest social adventure of the century."

Specifically, let us enroll in a mighty crusade for the Eighteenth Amendment and for personal sobriety and law observance as many young people as there are members in our societies and unions.

Forward for World Peace

Fourth, Crusade with Christ for World Peace. The last world journeys of Francis E. Clark were made in the interest of international good will. The Christian Endeavor movement is an adventure in human brotherhood. I commend to you tonight the proposal of our Crusade Commission for a Christian Endeavor disarmament petition. Believing that the coming International Disarmament Conference presents a major opportunity of the present generation, let us as young citizens respectfully call upon our government to take leadership with a definite program for the reduction of armaments.

In Kansas City we pledged our sacred honor to the fulfillment of the ideals and covenants of the Pact of Paris. We believe that this pact implies a decisive curtailment in armed forces of the nations. Patriotism begins at home, *but it does not end at home.* Love of country can best be exemplified when we work so that our nation may live in relationships of peace with all other nations.

Let us in this convention sign two mighty petitions and carry them back to all our unions and societies,—one petition for the observance and enforcement of the Eighteenth Amendment and for liberty with law, and another petition for America's leadership in the disarmament of the world.

Tonight I see again that vast audience on the closing night in Berlin. I watch the ocean of handkerchiefs—a white-capped sea. Again I am almost overpowered with the emotions that, tide above tide, sweep over us when the flags change hands. Tonight we revive those memories; more—we move on into a new sense of obligation, obligation inspired by those memories.

The world promised her sons and daughters that thes Great War was the war to end war. The world promised too much. Wars are not ended in war. But the vow stands, and peace is the time. Today the crusade begins anew. From this convention, from this hour, the International Society of Christian Endeavor is for disarmament, is for adherence to the World Court, is for the outlawry of armed conflict—aye, and for every other agency and enterprise that represents even a gesture of international good will.

Peace is precious. Its price must be paid accordingly. Peace must be won, won as war itself has always been won—if any war has ever been won—won by sacrifice, won by daring, won by risking much, won by being willing to give all.

These, then, are the goals:

Crusade with Christ to Win a Million Youths to Christ in these next two years.
Crusade with Christ for Christ and the Church.
Crusade with Christ for Citizenship.
Crusade with Christ for World Peace.

Finally, the first is last. It must be first tonight. must be first, because every good presented, every call sounded, and the result of all our endeavor stand or fall upon the surrender and dedication of the individual. To win others to Him, I must myself possess Him. Before I can do, I must be. Evangelism, service for and with the church, citizenship, peace—all of these, under God, must win or lose within my soul and by the measure of my spiritual success or failure.

It was a little man, a frail and punished man, a despised, rejected, alien man, a Roman Jew, a citizen of two worlds, who said, "I can do all things"—evangelism, citizenship, peace—all things. Was he a vain boaster, or did he have justification for his amazing boast? He is justified: the history of the world for nearly eighteen hundred years is the vindication of Paul's triumphant declaration of power. But let us complete Paul's declaration of power—"I can do all things *through Christ*": *This is the conclusion of the whole matter.*

Centuries ago a lawyer came to the Galilean and said, "I will follow thee whithersoever thou goest." Christian Endeavorers of North America, are we ready to say that? Trusting in the Lord Jesus Christ for strength, are we ready, are we ready to say that? If we are, we too can do all things. Not to follow Him is to stumble off into the dark of defeat, is to fall into failure. But through Christ with every goal that we may set, through Christ we shall win through.

> We thank Thee, Father, for the man
> Who gave our movement birth,
> Who caught the genius of the plan,
> And led it through the earth.
>
> We count our fifty golden years,
> Their triumph and their praise;
> We join the chorus of the cheers
> That youthful millions raise.
>
> We stand upon the rock of faith
> And cast our eyes afar
> Where leads the Galilean's path
> Beyond the plains of war.
>
> We lift our faces in the sun,
> We claim the world for truth
> We pledge our lives to things undone
> With Christ the King of youth.

A prayer of dismissal by Rev. Lapsley A. McAfee, D. D., with the benediction following, closed the session.

Not many hours hence, the young people of the convention were to meet at the Lord's Table, continuing in that symbolism a recognition of Him who is Saviour and Leader of youth, and who summons us to greater and ever greater service in His name.

THE GOLDEN JUBILEE COMMUNION SERVICE

Sunday, July 12, 8 A. M.

ORDER OF SERVICE

"This do in remembrance of Me"

INVOCATION AND LORD'S PRAYER (in unison) *standing*

CHORALE

RESPONSIVE LESSON—Psalm 103

Bless the Lord, O my soul: and all that is within me, bless his holy name.

Bless the Lord, O my soul: and forget not all his benefits:

Who forgiveth all thine iniquities; who healeth all thy diseases;

Who redeemeth thy life from destruction; who crowneth thee with loving-kindness and tender mercies;

Who satisfieth thy mouth with good things: so that thy youth is renewed like the eagle's.

The Lord executeth righteousness and judgment for all that are oppressed.

He made known his ways unto Moses; his acts unto the children of Israel.

The Lord is merciful and gracious; slow to anger, and plenteous in mercy.

He will not always chide; neither will he keep his anger for ever.

He hath not dealt with us after our sins; nor rewarded us according to our iniquities.

For as the heaven is high above the earth, so great is his mercy toward them that fear him.

As far as the east is from the west, so far hath he removed our transgressions from us.

Like as a father pitieth his children, so the Lord pitieth them that fear him.

For he knoweth our frame: he remembereth that we are dust.

As for man, his days are as grass: as a flower of the field, so he flourisheth.

For the wind passeth over it, and it is gone; and the place thereof shall know it no more.

But the mercy of the Lord is from everlasting to everlasting upon them that fear him: and his righteousness unto children's children;

To such as keep his covenant: and to those that remember his commandments to do them.

The Lord hath prepared his throne in the heavens: and his kingdom ruleth over all.

Bless the Lord, ye his angels, that excel in strength: that do his commandments, hearkening unto the voice of his word.

Bless the Lord, all ye his hosts: ye ministers of his, that do his pleasure.

Bless the Lord all his works in all places of his dominion: bless the Lord, O my soul.

HYMN—"How firm a foundation" (*standing*)

> How firm a foundation, ye saints of the Lord,
> Is laid for your faith in His excellent word!
> What more can he say than to you he hath said,—
> You who unto Jesus for refuge have fled?
> Fear not, I am with thee, O be not dismayed,
> For I am thy God, and will still give thee aid:
> I'll strengthen thee, help thee, and cause thee to stand,
> Upheld by My righteous, omnipotent hand.
>
> The soul that on Jesus hath leaned for repose,
> I will not, I will not desert to his foes;
> That soul, though all hell should endeavor to shake,
> I'll never, no never, no never forsake.

PRAYER

HYMN—"Beneath the Cross of Jesus" (*seated*)

> Beneath the cross of Jesus
>   I fain would take my stand,
> The shadow of a mighty rock
>   Within a weary land:
> A home within the wilderness,
>   A rest upon the way,
> From the burning of the noon-tide heat
>   And the burden of the day.
>
> Upon the cross of Jesus,
>   Mine eye at times can see
> The very dying form of One
>   Who suffered there for me:
> And from my smitten heart with tears
>   These wonders I confess;
> The wonder of his glorious love,
>   And my unworthiness.
>
> I take, O Cross, thy shadow
>   For my abiding-place;
> I ask no other sunshine than
>   The sunshine of His face;
> Content to let the world go by,
>   To know no gain nor loss,
> My sinful self my only shame,
>   My glory all the cross.

THE SACRAMENT OF THE LORD'S SUPPER

The Words of Institution

Prayer of Institution (*unison*)

Most gracious God, the Father of our Lord Jesus Christ, whose once offering up of Himself upon the cross, we commemorate before Thee; we earnestly desire Thy fatherly goodness to accept this our sacrifice of praise and thanksgiving:

And we pray Thee to bless and sanctify with Thy Word and Spirit these Thine own gifts of Bread and Wine which we set before Thee, that we may receive by faith Christ crucifi d for us, and so feed upon Him that He may be made one with us and we with Him.

And here we offer and present unto Thee ourselves, our souls and bodies, to be a reasonable, holy and living sacrifice unto Thee: praying that all we, who are partakers of this Holy Communion, may find that in this place Thou givest peace;

Through Jesus Christ our Lord; to whom with Thee and the Holy Spirit, be the glory and the praise, both now and evermore. Amen.

The Administering of the Bread

The Administering of the Cup

Prayer of Thanksgiving and Consecration (*unison*)

Almighty God, our Heavenly Father, we thank Thee for this holy hour. Thou hast brought us to Thy banqueting house and Thy banner over us is love. We have been refreshed in spirit by the presence of Thy Son, our living Lord, whose victorious death we have commemorated. We have come from all the corners of our nation and from many churches and homes but we are all one in Him. We thank Thee for our precious fellowship in Him and with each other. As we go upon our way we would consecrate ourselves anew to the service of our fellow men in Jesus' name. We would go forth under the sign of His Cross to fight the good fight of faith and to endure to the end.

May Thy kingdom of righteousness, goodwill and peace come among all men. May all injustice and evil be overthrown. Send us forth in the power of Thy Holy Spirit to do even "greater things than these" according to our Master's promise. And to Thee, Father, Son and Holy Spirit, one God, will we ascribe everlasting praise, world without end. Amen.

HYMN—"O Jesus, I have promised" (*standing*)

O Jesus, I have promised
  To serve Thee to the end:
Be thou forever near me,
  My Master and my Friend;
I shall not fear the battle
  If Thou art by my side,
Nor wander from the pathway
  If Thou wilt be my Guide.

O let me feel Thee near me,
  The world is ever near:
I see the sights that dazzle,
  The tempting sounds I hear;
My foes are ever near me,
  Around me and within;
But, Jesus, draw Thou nearer,
  And shield my soul from sin.

O Jesus, Thou hast promised
  To all who follow Thee,
That where Thou art in glory
  There shall Thy servant be;
And, Jesus, I have promised
  To serve Thee to the end;
O give me grace to follow,
  My Master and my Friend.

BENEDICTION AND MIZPAH (*unison*)

Morton

A View of the Convention in Session, Showing a Part of the Vast Audience

CHAPTER III

A DAY OF HIGH PURPOSES
Sunday, July 12

Youth Gathers at the Lord's Table—Christian Endeavor
Leaders in Many San Francisco Pulpits—Dr. Matthews
Commends Militant Prohibition—Raymond
Robins Speaks on "Power for
the Christian"

CHRISTIAN ENDEAVORERS in the International Golden
Jubilee Convention found joy in uniting in the most intimate, tender, inspiring rite of the church universal, the cele-
bration of holy communion. Five thousand young people, members of churches near and churches distant, communicants of at
least two score denominational bodies, shared in this period of
worship and recommital.

San Franciscans furnished the music of the service, with
Rev. Lawrance J. Mitchell at the console of the auditorium
organ.

The sacrament was administered by Dr. Daniel A. Poling,
Reformed Church; Dr. William Hiram Foulkes, Presbyterian
Church; Dr. A. E. Cory, Christian Church; and Dr. Lapsley
A. McAfee, Presbyterian Church. Serving the elements were
eighty-five elders drawn from a score of Protestant denominations. The front of the auditorium had been transformed over-
night so that a genuine churchly atmosphere, well suited to the
service, was given.

Heartstrings of "united youth" vibrated to the sweet sol-
emnity of the hour. It was a crowning devotional high light,
following close upon the splendid climax of enthusiasm and
recommital in the keynote convention session of Saturday evening.

The order of service, given in preceding pages, had been
prepared by Dr. Foulkes, with the co-operation of his associates.
Dr. Foulkes was to make again and again in this Golden Jubilee
Convention a deep impression on the devotional life of the
delegates. The Quiet Hour services, held at a similar period
in the four days that followed, grew in attendance and in universal appeal as the convention continued.

The San Francisco communion service recalled to many the two simultaneous services in the greatest church edifices of Germany—the one for the delegates from Germany, the other in the Dom, the church of the kaisers, for the visitors from other lands. This had been an unforgettable experience for the thousands of American, Canadian, British, and other delegates from all parts of the world, who shared in the Berlin World's Christian Endeavor Convention of 1930.

Guest Speakers in San Francisco Churches

Many of the leaders and speakers in the convention were heard Sunday morning and Sunday noon in the principal churches of San Francisco.

Dr. Poling preached at Temple Methodist Episcopal Church, which is the sponsoring institution of the Hotel William Taylor, the official hotel of the convention, facing the Civic Centre.

Dr. Poling and Dr. A. E. Cory, director of the Disciples of Christ pension fund, joined Sunday noon in laying the cornerstone of the new educational plant of the West Side Christian Church.

Dr. William Hiram Foulkes spoke at St. John's Presbyterian Church. Rev. Stanley B. Vandersall, Christian vocations superintendent of the International Society, was the morning preacher at the First Presbyterian Church.

Among other pulpit assignments were: At First Baptist Church, Colonel Raymond Robins; at Glide Memorial Methodist Episcopal Church, Rev. Charles F. Evans, field representative of the International Society; Rev. R. P. Anderson, editorial secretary, at the Hamilton Methodist Church; and at Calvary Presbyterian Church, Homer Rodeheaver, the convention song leader.

The Sunday Afternoon Session

It was an inspiring sight merely to look over the great audience of thousands that had flowed into the auditorium by 2.30 Sunday afternoon for the second general session of the convention. After an organ recital by Rev. Lawrance J. Mitchell, the song leader, Homer Rodeheaver, ushered in a thrilling period of song. The weather of Sunday afternoon was delightful, cool, and pleasant, and it says much for the earnestness of the young people that they attended in such crowds.

Harry N. Holmes, president of the New York State Christian Endeavor Union conducted the devotional service. He told of a native Christian Endeavor traveling secretary, who visited the leader of a group of churches in the heart of China.

"Stay with me a week and help me," said the leader. "But I cannot break my schedule," replied the secretary. "You must!" was the reply. "My church is a Christian Endeavor

church. We have seventy branch churches and every one has
a society. My own church has sixteen hundred members, and
most of them are Endeavorers. You *must* stay and help me."
What a testimony to the universal usefulness of this movement!

REV. MARK A. MATTHEWS
Pastor, First Presby-
terian Church,
Seattle

DR. A. E. CORY
Director of the Pension
Fund of the Dis-
ciples of Christ

It was a pastor who has more than thirty Christian Endeavor
societies in his church and its mission branches who was next
to speak. Dr. Mark A. Matthews, pastor of the First Presbyterian Church, Seattle, Wash., white-haired, tall, forceful, gave
one of the best factual addresses on national prohibition that
we have heard. There was enough of humor in the address to
season it well and to delight his audience.

THE CASE FOR PROHIBITION

Selections from an Address by Dr. Mark A. Matthews

The question now before this country is whether or not the people
are loyal to the Constitution. There is but one dividing line. We are
Constitutionalists, or we are personal libertyists. We believe in the
Constitution as the charter of our liberties, or we believe in satisfying
our appetites and therefore demand personal license. We believe in
liberty under law or we believe in license regardless of law. There
is no such thing as personal liberty. The only liberty possible is
liberty under law.

The agitation is revolving around the Eighteenth Amendment, because certain political forces antagonistic to liberty under law are
advocating the repeal of this amendment. The purpose of the Eighteenth Amendment is to prohibit the manufacture, sale, transportation,
importation, and exportation of intoxicating beverages. The Eighteenth
Amendment does not say that a man should not drink. It does not
say that it is a violation of law to take a drink. It does not say
that it is a sin to take a drink of intoxicating beverage. But it does
undertake to prohibit the manufacture and sale of intoxicating beverages.

Is there anybody who can truthfully say that the saloon, the distillery, and the brewery produced sobriety, prosperity, peace, happiness, or temperance in this country? I challenge America or the world to find any spot on earth where the distillery, the brewery, the saloon, the wine room, and the beer garden ever advocated temperance, obedience to law, righteousness, sobriety, or Christianity!

What Prohibition Did Not Do

Prohibition under the Eighteenth Amendment did not produce the bootlegger. He began to thrive in Massachusetts and other parts of this country one hundred and fifty years ago. He came into existence when the groceryman and dry goods merchant were permitted to sell wine and beer. Prohibition did not produce the moonshiner. He came into existence when this government taxed alcoholic beverages.

Prohibition did not produce the speakeasy. This was a product of the saloon. The man who conducted the speakeasy or blind pig bought a barrel of whiskey from the saloon, adulterated it, multiplied it into three or four barrels, and sold it right under the shadow of the saloon. In every town where there were saloons there were at least as many speakeasies, blind pigs, and blind tigers, as there were saloons.

Prohibition did not originate home brew. The farmer made his hard cider during saloon days; the family made blackberry wine, grape wine, and persimmon beer during saloon days. Education, enlightenment of conscience, public opinion, common decency, and social responsibility are destroying even these things.

The law can be enforced, and it is being enforced. All official records prove that fact. Mistakes have been made in law enforcement. They were made because the first appointees were political appointees, and in many instances corrupt men were entrusted with the duty of enforcing the law. They were brutal, unreasonable, and illegal in their practices. We have lately enforced the statute against beer ninety per cent; against wine, eighty per cent; and against hard liquors, seventy-five per cent. The law can be enforced. It will be enforced.

You cannot have the advanced, efficient mechanical and scientific age that we now have and get along with the breweries and the distilleries.

Which do you want?

Do you want the manufacturing plants of productive industry, the churches, the schools? Or do you vote for the brewery, the beer-garden, and the saloon?

Do you want the boulevard, the happy home, educated children, industrious husbands, and contented wives? You have these, and can have them more abundantly with the progress of prohibition.

At the conclusion of Dr. Matthews' address, the delegates unanimously adopted a prohibition and law enforcement resolution which gathered up the main thought of his speech. Support of prohibition even if it takes fifty years to bring it to success! Such was the spirit of the resolution, presented by Harry N. Holmes, chairman of the resolutions committee. The complete statement is given in another chapter.

Well-Attended Prayer Meetings

Soon after adjournment of the afternoon mass-meeting, the delegates gathered for six simultaneous prayer-meetings, held in various halls of the auditorium and in Temple Church.

The following were the leaders: W. Roy Breg, Southern secretary of the International Society; Carroll M. Wright, financial secretary and travel superintendent; Stanley B. Vandersall, Christian vocations superintendent; Rev. E. L. Reiner, Chicago, International Society trustee; Alvin J. Shartle, treasurer and field-secretary; and Mrs. Francis E. Clark.

Mrs. Clark's meeting was a particularly happy and gracious reception of the mother of Christian Endeavor by Junior superintendents to the number of about two hundred.

A Session of Powerful Messages

Soon after the opening of Sunday evening's convention song service, Homer Rodeheaver led in the singing of two of Charles H. Gabriel's hymns, and then presented Mr. Gabriel, a Californian, who received an ovation.

One of the fine features of the convention was the series of short addresses by young people on the problems and outlooks of youth. The first of these was given to the crowd that thronged the auditorium on Sunday night. Miss Mary E. Babcock, of Occidental College, Los Angeles, is a winsome and thoughtful personality. Several paragraphs are quoted from her splendid message.

CHRIST AND YOUTH

By Mary E. Babcock

We, the youth of today, like to be called modern youth. We like to be considered independent and self-sufficient—quite well able to take care of ourselves, to find our way about.

But even so, those of us who know Christ, humbly, yes, and gladly acknowledge the need of Him both for ourselves and for those other modern young people who do not know Him.

Youth needs Christ as a very present Guide in everyday living. Youth is not so much concerned with one's eternal salvation, as with strength to lead a Christian life daily.

I asked a group of high-school boys and girls to tell me honestly why they personally needed Jesus. That they spoke frankly may perhaps be judged by their words, which I quote almost exactly. One boy said, "I need Him to keep me from copying a Latin paper." Another said, "If you ask Him to help you, you don't even want to cheat." A girl flung out, "He keeps me from being three times worse as a grouch than I am now." A boy, the athlete of the crowd, said, "He helps me not to slug a guy in a basketball game when the referee isn't looking."

One girl told me that she needed Christ to help her to befriend a girl who is shunned by the rest of the crowd at school. Practical needs, aren't they?

But Jesus' teaching concerned itself mostly with practical things. Then I asked those boys and girls, "Well, isn't Jesus, the Teacher, the Example, sufficient to meet your need of Him?" And I was glad when they answered, without hesitation, "No!"—and told me that they needed Christ, the Son of God, in His full divine power and guidance.

Because youth needs Christ to give meaning and purpose to a life of confusion, to guide in practical right living, and to be a Saviour for now and for eternity, the youth of the world must know Christ. They will know Him best in the winning of youth by youth, and not by testimony of words so much as by every day Christian living.

Rev. Morris H. Turk, D. D., pastor of the Williston Congregational Church of Portland, Me., where Christian Endeavor was formed, brought Golden Jubilee greetings from "the best known and best loved of all Protestant churches in the world."

A Movement—Moving Forward

The next speaker was Hon. Curtis D. Wilbur of San Francisco, former United States Secretary of the Navy, and now judge of the United States Circuit Court. He is a former Christian Endeavorer, and showed his interest in the convention in a number of ways.

"Christian Endeavor is still a movement, and it is moving forward," said Judge Wilbur. The speaker made happy reference to the attractive silk panels in the ceiling and side walls of the convention hall. One panel shows battleships entering a harbor, while another is a spirited representation of the frigate "Constitution,"—"Old Ironsides." Mr. Wilbur mentioned that he met his wife at the 1897 International Christian Endeavor Convention in San Francisco. He recalled a portion of the address of Dr. John Willis Baer given then.

He continued:

"Endeavorers have been building a world of new ideas and ideals. Think of the accomplishments of these years since our last convention here. In my own profession, the law, we find woman enfranchised, jury qualifications broadened, criminal law humanized, probation and parole well recognized, and juvenile delinquency treated as a social problem. There are detention homes, extended compulsory education, laws to protect the child and the woman worker. In international law, we have clarified our codes and rules, established a great World Court, and made treaties of naval limitation.

"We are endeavoring to present Christian principles—Christian Endeavor principles, in fact—even in the fabric of the law, which changes less readily than many things in modern life."

A Tribute to Peacemakers

Judge Wilbur spoke with feeling of the work for peace of such statesmen as Hon. Frank B. Kellogg, now a justice of the World Court. "The court, which Mr. Kellogg through the Paris Pact of Peace helped to make more necessary to us, is a fine new tool for international co-operation. Our prayer tonight as Christian Endeavorers must be for those who, as peacemakers in all the realms of life, are truly rendering service for Christ and the church."

Judge Wilbur's wife and son were introduced. The 1897 Convention delegates present were asked to stand and more than one hundred responded. They were given hearty applause by the audience that now filled the auditorium to bursting.

Colonel Raymond Robins' address, which followed, concluding the evening session, made a profound impression. Colonel Robins won his audience from the first word. The hall was breathless in suspense as he spoke.

POWER FOR THE CHRISTIAN

Selections from the Address by Colonel Raymond Robins

"As many as received Him to them gave He power."

What about religion, anyway? Why not build laboratories rather than churches? Isn't chemistry of more consequence to the world than religion? Is religion anything beyond words, forms, and traditions?

Millions of young people ask these questions and answer them to the effect that religion is a survival, an outworn appendage, a fast-declining force in life. One great nation in its entirety is committed to materialism and science rather than to religion and Christianity.

Never before has there been an hour when authority and precedent had less power, and when adventure and questioning had more.

I would take you to the most crowded quarter of the West End in Chicago. There in a space one mile square, 75,000 people speaking thirty-one languages, lived when I first came to that city. Thirty years ago I had come from the Northland, fired with the power of fellowship with Jesus Christ, with a sense of obligation, a hunger for beauty, and the feeling that I held power in trust.

In that neighborhood many groups sought to make human life better, either by economic or political reforms.

It seemed as if we must have something in common, although I felt that religion was the power required to make life more endurable and liberty within reach, while they trusted in the ballot box or the teachings of Karl Marx. Grey-blooded children were in those streets. The police officers on their beats were allied with vice and crime. Could we that cared about these things do team work? Because of the differences that divided us, no one made a real dent on this ward.

When we came together, we found to the surprise of some that we could agree on two points: first, that the future of this neighborhood was in the control of its 22,000 children; second, that the first need of these Chicago children was for daily bread.

Attacking the Wide Front

We fed the children. But we found that quality of food counted more than quantity. When the milk we bought for them was impure, we were not solving their problem. We sent twenty-three samples of milk, bought in the open market and sealed and labeled, to a chemist. Nineteen of the twenty-three showed that they contained formalin; here was old milk that had been treated to make it salable. We found the cure for that.

Bad meat was trailed to the stock yards. And we put into Joliet Penitentiary the crooked chief inspector and six of his assistants,— fourteen in all having been indicted.

But I don't expect to solve social problems by putting men in jail.

Our influence extended to Washington. Dr. Harvey Wiley told us that it was our testimony, as much as any other recognizable factor, that caused Congress to pass the Pure Food and Drug Act.

We went on. Industrial unrest and bad factory conditions injured the home life of these children who were now being fed.

Then the strike came—a hard school kept for those who won't learn elsewhere. For eight weeks in winter, 40,000 garment workers we kept from starving. Finally a trade agreement was made that has been the basis for similar agreements all over the country.

There was still trouble in these homes we were watching. The breadwinner, leaving the shop with his pay, left at the saloon resources that were needed to feed the home. Gambling, vice, and licentiousness were rampant, and each drained the social health of these children and their homes. There was one thing we could not do without in our planning—and that was religion. Only pure, uncorrupted Christianity could really transform this situation. The best that economics and politics could do was not enough.

No Power without Religion

Australia has made great economic strides under her labor program. There has been no child labor there for twenty years. The people largely control their government. Arduous labor has been restricted to eight hours a day. The only eight-hour-day monument in the world is in Melbourne, erected largely by popular subscription. But Sydney is more drunken than any cities I know except Glasgow, and Whitechapel, London. I found whole communities with the "get-rich-quick" conscience. In Australia the government itself ran a huge lottery. There was complete lapse of moral quality. The church had no influence on labor.

I tell you there is no constant progress and no final triumph in attempts at world regeneration that do not include the world regenerator, Jesus Christ.

Germany in 1913 did some things better than any other people. Even in war, and by her virtue rather than by vice, she held the world at bay for four years on four fronts. Berlin and Westphalia gave the worker more rights and greater security than most countries. Unemployment had ceased to be a problem. Conservation, such as America has never known, was the rule. In the Black Forest, I have seen men cutting timber where timber has been cut for seven hundred years. The Rhineland gave forty bushels of wheat to the acre—and the same land was giving wheat before Christ died on Calvary.

Practical matters, yes! And Germany in those days stopped there. "Why talk religion to *educated* men?" asked one of my hearers. How is Germany tonight? Sorrow in every home. Tribute due to foreign masters. Is religion necessary?

In prayer there is strength for the strong. Luther prayed, and stood, one man against his world. Cromwell, seeing defeat on three fields, formed an army of men "with the fear of God, and God only, in their hearts," and his army fought fifty-four engagements without a single defeat.

Let us have faith in a universe that has produced Jesus Christ and Paul, Luther, Joan of Arc, Florence Nightingale! Fulfill in each one of us thy holy will. Give us the power that comes to men who surrender only to Jesus Christ.

So closed one of the great days of the convention, a day of inspiration, of vision, and of power.

MR. PAUL SHOUP
*General Chairman, Conven-
tion Committee; President
Southern Pacific Railroad*

MR. FRED D. PARR
*Associate Chairman, Con-
vention Committee*

DR. FRED B. FISHER
*Former Methodist Bishop
of India who delivered
stirring addresses on
the closing day of
the Convention*

CHAPTER IV

CHRIST FOR THE WORLD'S NEEDS

Monday, July 13

The "School of the Convention" Opens—Our
Responsibility to Make Christ Known—
Probing the Soul of Modern Asia

FOR a number of the leaders, this convention day began at
seven o'clock, when the first of four daily breakfast conferences for all leaders of the convention was held in the cheery
dining room of the Hotel William Taylor. More than one
hundred leaders of conferences and chairmen of conferences
met with President Poling and Secretary Sherwood, for inspiration, consultation and instruction, at this early hour, day
after day. Beginning Tuesday, the faculty heard each day
a statement by Dr. Harry Thomas Stock, conference counsellor,
and others, regarding the points and issues suggested and raised
in the first-period conference theme of the morning.

The faculty joined increasing numbers of delegates at the
daily Quiet Hour meeting, led by Rev. William Hiram Foulkes,
D. D., vice-president of the International Society of Christian
Endeavor and pastor of Old First Presbyterian Church, Newark,
N. J. "Mountain Peaks with the Master" was Dr. Foulkes'
topic for Monday morning. This message, and others of the
series, are reviewed in a short chapter devoted to the Quiet
Hour meetings of the convention.

Enthusiasm for the Conference Idea

Extensive preparation had been made, as to subject matter,
personnel, age grouping, and places of meeting, that the conference program of the Golden Jubilee Convention should be
typical of Christian Endeavor at its best. A grouping of topics,
leaders, and conferees seems to have been achieved that successfully blended educational power, practical information, and religious inspiration. We believe that few conference sessions
have been so richly blessed as were these.

The delegates did not conceal their enthusiasm. They entered happily into the two-period arrangement, by which each
delegate shared for the first fifty-five minutes in the discussion
of a major religious and social theme (which for the first day
was "Sharing Christ with Others"), and in the second period
discussed under other leaders the principles and methods of
many forms of church activities.

A separate chapter is devoted to the details of this splendid plan, with specimen material from some of the forty conference sessions held daily.

"See Through Jesus' Eyes"

Now the delegates gather for a morning mass-meeting in the auditorium, opened promptly at 11.15 o'clock with song. Alvin J. Shartle presides.

The theme of the session is, "I, if I be lifted up . . ." and the first speaker is Rev. Jesse M. Bader, D. D., secretary of evangelism and head of home-mission work for the Disciples of Christ. His topic is "The World's Need."

Arrestingly he began; "Jesus shed tears twice—once over a dead man, and once over Jerusalem. He wept not over the physical condition of the city, but for its people. For he looked always beyond buildings—and saw people. We must follow this example, looking through the eyes of Jesus, and with His heart-beat in us."

Jesus saw people who were hungry, as we see many today, said the speaker. There are needs of food, of education, and of spiritual life. It is still true that the hearts of men are restless until they rest in God. We must bring Jesus, who is big enough to meet the need of all mankind. He is the revelation of what God is; what man, through Him, may become.

The speaker outlined our responsibility to make Christ known. "We have been ringing church bells when we ought to be ringing door bells. Our motto should be, 'We tell it. They believe it. Christ does it.' Are you clerk or salesman? The clerk waits till the customer comes to him. The salesman goes out hunting for the customer."

Illustrating how evangelism is simply sharing Christ, Dr. Bader told of the famine in Ireland in 1845, when America, hearing of the need, sent over food to feed the dying. Suppose America had been deaf to the call! Well, we have the bread of life. We have the water of life. And the world is hungry and thirsty. What shall we do about it? "I believe we have enough power in the Christian Endeavor movement," continued the speaker, "if we can set the young people aflame, to set the church afire and bring back the days of the first century."

Theodore Roosevelt was taken when a small boy to visit a cathedral which he was told was the house of God. He appeared to be afraid, and his father asked him the reason. The boy said, "Where do they keep the zeal?" The father wanted to know where he got that idea, and the child replied that the minister had spoken a week or two before on the theme, "The zeal of thine house hath eaten me up." It is a fair question. Where do we keep the zeal? The King would speak through us. Are we willing to let Him speak?

The Task in the Local Church

"The Task in the Local Church" was the topic of the address that followed, the speaker being Rev. Frank D. Getty, director of young people's work in the Presbyterian Church, U. S. A. He began by quoting John R. Mott's incisive words.

AN IOWA GROUP IN GOLDEN-JUBILEE PARADE

"*The need is the call.*" We had heard a statement of the world's need. Now what?

Imagine a calm evening in Galilee, down by the lakeside. Thousands of hungry people are there and Jesus commands His disciples, "Give ye them to eat." This word expresses our responsibility today. How are we answering that call?

In reading our Bibles we should learn to vitalize the stories we read by the use of our imagination. Reconstruct the scene. Here are the disciples. They are quite incapable of meeting the needs of these people. And then a boy is brought to the Master. What is this he has? Just a lunch put up by a loving mother. "Will you let me use it?" asks Jesus, and the boy hands it over. With it Jesus feeds the multitude. He is asking us today to let Him use what we have. Are we willing?

Mr. Getty gave a number of illustrations of young people who were fired with new zeal through a study of evangelism and by realizing that Jesus could work through them. Our need

is not to find something to do for Christ, but to let Him work
through us. He will do the drawing; He will attract men to
Himself. Begin in evangelism by talking religion with your
friends, the speaker advised.

Greetings from W. C. T. U.

Miss Lenadell Wiggins, of Pennsylvania, brought greetings
from the National Women's Christian Temperance Union, paying tribute to Christian Endeavor, which raises the standards
of morality wherever societies are formed. She urged the
signing of a monster Youth Roll supporting the Eighteenth
Amendment, which will be sent in December to President
Hoover as a definite expression of youth on this issue. Local
chapters of the W. C. T. U. have charge of the enrollment.

Convention "On the Air"

Radio played an important part in the influence of the
Christian Endeavor Convention, locally and nationally. President Poling is famed as a national radio speaker and the man-
agement of Radio Station KPO was pleased to present him
each noon, beginning Monday, to a' Pacific Coast audience.
Judged by newspaper and other comments, many listened in,
and came to know Dr. Poling and Christian Endeavor more
personally in the daily conference. On Thursday, the whole
nation was to listen while President Herbert Hoover spoke from
Washington by radio, widely broadcast, to the Golden Jubilee
Convention young people.

Paul Pitman, director of KPO, attended each noon, and introduced Dr. Poling.

The radio talks are quoted in a later chapter. Monday
afternoon's denominational rallies are also reported briefly elsewhere.

Crusading Spirit in Evening Session

The missionary spirit of the day's services continued with
the evening session, in which Asia's Christian outlook was
capably presented by gifted speakers.

The preliminaries, too, were of real value. Homer Rodeheaver and C. A. Lehmann, of Chicago, assistant song director,
led chorus and audience in a host of songs. "Greater Things
than These" has become a convention favorite. The crowds
have become well-acquainted with the new book "New Hymnal
for Christian Youth," and its popularity increases. Every
delegate has received a copy of the Golden Jubilee Edition,
which has just come from the press.

Forty voices from Hawaii were heard in special numbers.
Rev. Akaika Akana, Hawaiian president, introduced the chorus
and brought the islands' greetings to Dr. Poling, Mrs. Clark,

and the convention. There were leis—the brilliant garlands of the Polynesians and Hawaiians—for several convention leaders.

The Call to Christian Citizenship

The youth speaker of the evening was Robert Ropp, national chairman of Allied Youth, one of the four divisions of the new Allied Forces movement for prohibition and law observance.

Mr. Ropp spoke, in part, as follows:

The time has come for youth to march. The Holy Sepulchre is about to be wrested from their hands by an ancient and treacherous foe. Our task in defending the Constitution of the United States against the lawless attack of the liquor forces is not less vital nor dramatic than ancient efforts to recapture the Holy City.

At a conference of representative young people called by Dr. Daniel A. Poling, and held in Pittsburgh on April 13, there was conceived a national campaign of Allied Youth. Officers of the National Council were there elected.

Allied Youth is an integral part of the Allied Forces for Prohibition, of which the other departments are: Allied Campaigners, Allied Business Men, and Allied Women.

The program of Allied Youth will go hand in hand with that of the Allied Campaigners, who take the field in September in support of the Eighteenth Amendment. We youth begin at once to enroll all young people who are ready to unite in defense of the Constitution and in support of national prohibition and liberty with law.

Allied Youth is not conceived as a competitive movement. It is agreed that in choosing the local council in any city, representation should be given to B. Y. P. U., Christian Endeavor, Epworth League, Luther League, and any societies of Jewish or Catholic young people or of a secular kind, that are definitely committed to the maintenance and enforcement of prohibition. The movement is non-sectarian and non-partisan. With the national council already in existence, local councils will complete the network. Thy dry youth of the nation will then have a voice with which to repudiate the false charge that all young people are against prohibition and are joining to make lawless attack upon it.

Wha⁺ is still more important, dry youth will have a medium through which to function as a constructive civic power.

We need for the campaign young men and young women in every State, and finally in every county and important centre, who will pledge with me to this high undertaking their faith, their loyalty, and their unwavering devotion. I summon *you* to this aggressive campaign. We have a cause and we must fight for it!

On Tiptoe, Fists Uplifted

Dr. Poling summoned the whole audience to its feet. Then, with right arms stretched upward, the hands clinched into fists, and each person rising on tiptoe, the great audience repeated in unison, "Trusting in the Lord Jesus Christ for strength, I will see this thing through."

Then the field secretaries were introduced, a splendid crowd, heartily cheered. Howard L. Brown, field-secretary of the California Christian Endeavor Union, who is also president of the Field-Secretaries' Union, joined with President Poling in these presentations.

The full-time officers of the International Society were introduced. These men—Sherwood, Vandersall, Shartle, Hamilton, Wright, and the regional field men, Evans, Brown, Breg and Singer—have invested their lives and their full powers for the promotion and abundant usefulness of the Christian Endeavor movement. Something of their crowded lives, their devotion to duty, and their unflinching loyalty to Christian ideals, was recognized by the Tuesday evening audience, which gave an ovation to one after another of these men. Without this leadership, a Golden Jubilee Convention would not have been a possibility.

Followed the award of Christian Endeavor World subscription banners. Wisconsin Union won the first prize, and Clifford Earle, State secretary, received the award amid applause.

Now we were to hear of India, on which the eyes of the world's intelligence are centred, and the message was brought by Rev. Edmund D. Lucas, D. D., president of Forman Christian College, Lahore, India.

New Tides in the World

"There is much to be said about India," said Dr. Lucas, "but there is much to be unsaid as well, and there are but few ways of saying aright what should be said."

Dr. Lucas has lived for twenty-three years in Lahore, loves India, and declares that he wishes to spend the rest of his life in his home city. He commanded rapt attention as he spoke of India's youth. "The youth of India," he declared, "faces the future and thinks of it as it is presented to them in the life of Mahatma Gandhi. India has been conquered many times. For 150 years Great Britain has controlled her destinies. In January of this year, however, Great Britain, moved by young India's insistent demand for self-government, said: 'If you agree on a definite plan of government, whatever it may be, you may have it.' That is a fair offer. But now that it has been made it remains to be seen whether or not India will let the desire of many years slip from her grasp.

"For the great problem confronting India today is the problem of the Hindoo and the Mohammedan. It is a problem that 1,500 years has not solved. In the past twelve months there has been bitter strife in every great Indian city, including Lahore. In view of that strife, when in Delhi, Gandhi said that he would fast twenty-one days—and fasting means fasting to Gandhi, and not merely a lighter diet—for he would as soon die as live in an India where Mohammedans and Hindus cannot live together in peace."

On the nineteenth day of his fast Gandhi called in Mr. Andrews (who thought the aged reformer was dying) and asked him to sing, "When I survey the wondrous cross on which the Prince of glory died.'' Where did Gandhi learn the lesson of vicarious suffering? Who taught him that a man may take upon himself the burden of his people's sin? There is only one who has ever really done this. Jesus! And Gandhi has learned this of Him.

For Freedom of Conscience

Dr. Lucas told how there had been written into the Magna Charta of new India the principle that no obstacle should be placed in the way of any man or woman that desired to follow his or her conscience, or that desired to change his or her religion, and that no one should be looked down upon because of caste or because of ancient prejudice.

Several great things stand out in Gandhi's life. There is his manifest sincerity. People trust him. He is the soul of truth. In India there are four classes on the trains. Third class is the poorest, and Gandhi always travels third class. He does this that he may completely identify himself with the people. When he travels on a mission he charges about ten cents a day for expenses. He identifies himself with the poorest of the poor. Some ask, "Why does Gandhi look so hungry?" The answer is that there are in India fifty million people hungrier than he is. He is one with others, even the lowest, and is willing even to die if that would save his people.

During recent disturbances Lord Irwin, the Viceroy, had a very difficult task. Night after night he and Gandhi were closeted for hours trying to find a solution of the problem that confronted them. Gandhi was asked how peace was attained. He answered, "It was goodness on the part of Lord Irwin, and, if I may say it without boasting, on my part too, and the practical application of the principles of Christ."

The missionaries in India are facing difficulties as never before. They have to live their lives in the light of a life like that of Gandhi who has lived and is living the life of Christ as we have never lived it. Missionaries live under keen and searching eyes.

Gandhi says, "I am searching for God." Can we say that we have really found Him? We should never have found Him without Jesus, and without a Christian mother and a Christian home.

On this day the Orient had its hour. The address of Dr. Lucas on India was followed by an eloquent address by Dr. C. Y. Cheng, of Shanghai, China, who is moderator of the United Christian Church in China. Speaking on "The Changing Orient," Dr. Cheng stated that he was inspired, impressed, and encouraged by the spirit of the Christian Endeavor Convention.

The Changing Orient

"We have been hearing so much about the change in America's attitude toward missions," he said, "that some of us had wondered, and were depressed by the possibility that American churches might give less and less of themselves toward Christianizing China. I am no longer depressed; I am joyous. While great numbers of young people, in Christian Endeavor and elsewhere in the church, feel as you do about missions and about Christ, I shall have no fear for America or China or any other country in the world."

It is youth's day in China, said Dr. Cheng. In the Northern government there is scarcely an important official over forty. A larger number of these than ever before are Christians.

The old haughty China has gone—and eager youth remains, testing all knowledge by practical and scientific means. Religion did not at first appeal to this spirit, for it could not be weighed or felt. But Dr. Cheng believes that the Christian church in China has turned the corner and is on a road that leads toward hope and fulfillment. Since reality is everything, shall not Christianity be judged in China by what it does to men rather than upon the theoretical statements of its traditions?

Turning toward Christ

Dr. Cheng believes that Chinese youth is now turning toward Christ. He mentioned two striking examples, also, of the interest that scholars of the New Thought Movement, even while attacking the church, have shown in the personality of Jesus Christ. It is the wholly sacrificial character of Christ, plus His recognition of the value of all men and women, that won one opponent of the church to admit that the One upon whom the church is founded is beyond attack.

Another scholar, considered an enemy of all religion, displays the pictures of many philosophers and leaders of religion in his study. In times of discouragement, it is to the face of Christ that this man turns his eyes, said Dr. Cheng.

The Chinese leader spoke slowly and clearly, without accent. He is a man of middle age, but his eyes are almost boyish and his face is full of expression and light.

Dr. Cheng has been one of the active leaders of Christian Endeavor in China and has helped to reorganize the union and correlate its activities with those of the United Church, which consists of fourteen denominations. During the Boxer uprising, his sister and brother-in-law were killed, as well as one hundred members of their church. Dr. Cheng studied in New York in 1922-1924. Since May, 1931, he has been traveling in the United States, and came directly from Connecticut to speak to the Golden Jubilee Convention.

CHAPTER V

CHRISTIAN YOUTH ON THE MARCH

Tuesday, July 14

A Christian Social Order Proposed—"Thousands of Clear-Eyed Youth" Parade on Market Street, Followed by Civic Centre Demonstration—Dr. MacTaggart and Harry N. Holmes Speak for Peace, Unity and Christian Advance

ANOTHER busy morning. Youth thronged the Quiet Hour service. The second day of the conferences (a test of the interest they had won from the delegates) showed increased attendances. The theme of the day was "Christian Citizenship and a Christian Social Order."

Harry Thomas Stock had made a splendid statement of the possibilities of this conference topic in the early-morning faculty session. At the 11.15 mass meeting, he extended these remarks into a notable address. He was introduced by Stanley B. Vandersall, chairman of the morning.

Dr. Stock is secretary of young people's work for the Congregational-Christian Churches (the newly merged denomination) and is regarded nationally as one of the leaders in this form of religious and educational leadership.

A CHRISTIAN SOCIAL ORDER

The older generation, through its inventions and discoveries, has made almost incomparable contributions to the life of the present and the future. But whether these will prove to be the ruin or the salvation of our civilization depends upon the quality of our moral ideals and the courage which the younger generation shows in controlling its life according to these ideals.

The concentration of business in a few hands, for instance, may mean either a new era of common justice for all who labor and use the products of labor, or a new privileged class and a new serfdom, which will issue in misery, revolution, and world confusion. It all depends upon the moral ideals which we profess and follow.

The machine can do the work of fifty men. This may mean a new leisure with a new appetite for the higher and deeper things of life. Or it may mean continuous unemployment and the subjection of the weak to the domination of a moneyed oligarchy. What happens depends upon the quality of our moral ideals. The ease of transportation has encouraged many of us to travel abroad. What a chance this is for the development of an international friendship! But when we go, as we so frequently do, with a contempt of European railroads, hotels, and food, and a vociferous pride in everything American, we bring both ourselves and our religion into disrepute.

Ill will or good will? It depends upon our attitudes, and these are an expression of our moral standards.

Youth's Freedom to Venture

Young people today have much more freedom from chaperonage than ever before. They have at their command powerful implements of speed. If they have developed ideals which control both mind and muscle, how gloriously strong an adulthood there will be tomorrow! But without such a control, how serious the injury to both the present and future generations!

The development of a controlling Christian morality for personal and social living is the greatest need of our times.

How shall we do this? Experimentation is the answer of the hour, and rightly understood this word is the key to the problem. No progress in medicine, sanitation, or political organization has come about without adventurous spirits who were dissatisfied with things as they are.

HARRY N. HOLMES
*Secretary, World Alliance
for International Friend-
ship through the
Churches*

HARRY THOMAS STOCK, D.D.
*Boston, Student Secretary,
Congregational Education
Society*

And what a challenge awaits us today! To create a society in which all persons are respected, regardless of color or nationality or age, to build a civilization in which the oncoming generations are not unwillingly and unwittingly enslaved by strong liquor, to construct an industrial and economic order in which the interests and rights of all are served, to create an international relationship in which the nations are committed to finding a way of co-operation without resorting to the primitive method of conflict—what a challenge to the spirit of pioneer and adventurer!

Experimentation is needed. But historical perspective is equally necessary. We learn everything by experience, but many of our most useful possessions have come to us through the experience of the race. To ignore the constantly attested truths of our social heritage, to experiment with explosives for the sake of proving what every sane observer already knows, that is sheer folly. There are virtues and vices; the results of virtue and of vice are well proved. Experiment for the sake of a higher good is sound moral policy, but experiment for the sake of "expressing myself" on the lowest level is both silly and ruinous.

Test Authority by Results

In moral matters, as in art and music and medicine, we should take the counsel of experts. In matters of living there are experts whose lives commend themselves by their beauty, nobility, and sincere unselfishness. These competent leaders may not be sophisticated novelists, or "smart Aleck" wielders of the pen; they may be untutored men and women whose influence in the community has been an abiding benediction. In them is reflected the spirit of Jesus Christ, and we who believe in Jesus dare to challenge the world to test His teachings, to observe His life. Is there anywhere a higher morality? Is there anywhere else the incarnation of such a morality?

By the test of the scientist himself Jesus stands before the ages as the great Expert in morality. By the test of the scientist He stands before us as the Revealer of the saving religion. The appeal to youth is likewise that of the scientist. Try this for yourself.

The session adjourned promptly at noon, to allow delegations to prepare for the convention parade. The young people were to leave the Civic area by 1.30 at the latest, so that all units could be in position in the streets converging on Market Street's eastern, or bay side, terminus at 2 o'clock.

The parade moved promptly at 2.30, thus vindicating the prediction of the chairman of the parade committee, Colonel Henry G. Mathewson.

For this one noon, Dr. Poling conducted the Youth Radio Conference from the studio of Station KPO. W. Roy Breg, Southern secretary of the International Society of Christian Endeavor, presided and read the delegates' questions that Dr. Poling answered at the conclusion of his address on "Youth and Christian Citizenship."

Crusaders on the March

The big event of Tuesday afternoon was the convention parade, which marched west on Market Street, one of America's broadest and busiest thoroughfares, from the Ferries to the Civic Centre.

This was a magnificent testimony to the enthusiasm of youth. And youth's Christian witness! For one business man remarked, as he watched the ranks go past, "I would not have believed it. I did not think there was as much faith in all the world."

From the beginning, the newspaper men and women had been alert, interested, and friendly. Some of their best news stories were written about this parade, and a portion of one, by Earl Berkeley, of *The San Francisco Chronicle*, is quoted here.

Thousands of clear-eyed, singing young Americans swept gayly up Market Street yesterday afternoon in another demonstration that religion is a potent force in this country.

The sweet, fresh faces, with that "back-home" look associated with so many memories for another generation, clustered in the march from out the hotels and quarters where these youths have been so conspicuous for nearly a week.

At city hall they formed a solid phalanx, they and their elders, until probably ten thousand were gathered in the civic centre. Then as a giant chorus, led by massed bands, they rolled out old, familiar hymns that stirred their great-grandfathers when the nation was struggling for life, songs that bulwarked their grandfathers in the Union and Confederate armies, and hymns of the later days.

And thousands who watched joined in these songs, some to sing a hymn for the first time in many years.

The Parade Begins

In this procession, led by seven policemen on horseback, half a dozen bands played. As one selection in brass ended, young voices were raised in songs of the States, cheers of the cities, and familiar hymns of the church. And the bands, when massed, played "Onward, Christian Soldiers," and other Christian marching-songs.

Mrs. Francis E. Clark, President and Mrs. Poling, and Dr. Foulkes were brought to the reviewing-stand in front of San Francisco's city hall by the large automobile that the municipality placed at their disposal throughout the convention.

Other officers of the International Society of Christian Endeavor marched at the head of the parade, followed by Wisconsin, whose front-rank position had been won by the efforts of Field-Secretary Clifford Earle and his associates in finance and in advance registrations for the 1931 Convention. Significant it is that Wisconsin invites and receives the 1933 International Christian Endeavor Convention for Milwaukee. This large delegation wore red and white, and struggling with a stiff wind, carried umbrellas.

"Trench Hats" for Penn State

Canvas hats made in the form of the trench hats or "tin hats" of the World War soldiers are worn by the men of Pennsylvania's delegation. It is a splendid group, more than one hundred strong, the larger number having come on the Golden Jubilee special, with Mrs. Clark, Dr. and Mrs. Poling and International Society leaders. The song-leader for William Penn's State is dressed in a flaming red jersey, and displays great energy.

New Jersey's splendid delegation wears the Princeton colors, orange and black. Cactus, recently seen "on the root" for the first time by some of the Eastern delegates, is represented by pasteboard copies carried by Arizona's youthful delegation. Colorado, in orchid capes, makes a splendid impression.

Open-Air Christian Endeavor Meeting at the Civic Centre, San Francisco, near the Exposition Auditorium, where the Golden Jubilee Convention met. At the conclusion of the parade this meeting was addressed by Mayor Angelo J. Rossi, of San Francisco.

George Washington and his wife march at the head of the District of Columbia's forces. Then come the Endeavorers of Idaho, the New Englanders led by the Puritan couple, and Minnesota. Missouri brings along the inevitable mule, protesting against the smart pace of the marchers. Montana girls and boys with "Powder River" sombreros, are cheered by the crowds along the curb. Nebraska's delegation uses red and yellow insignia to advantage.

New Mexico, too, has a mule. A large group from Illinois follows.

Then comes the Empire State, with blue capes and red feathers in the jaunty chapeaux. Ohio sings as it marches, a fine group from the city and State of the 1927 International Convention, Cleveland. Dixie carries banners, "Christian Endeavor Leads the World to Christ." Some are dressed in the picturesque garb of European peasants. Hawaii's forty delegates, in decorated trucks, play and sing, and are greeted with enthusiasm by the city that thinks of these Pacific islands as her own possession and playground. Some Japanese are in Hawaii's group.

Oregon Honors Dr. Poling

Oregon Christian Endeavorers presented a "moving pageant" of the life of Dr. Daniel A. Poling, who grew up in this great State of the Northwest. Several girls and boys wear the costume of the 1880's. A couple in this garb push a baby-carriage to represent Poling's birth and childhood. Delegates who march behind these pioneer types wear green blouses and berets, liberally decorated with yellow O's that stand for Oregon. Many watchers considered this the most striking feature of the parade, which now filled Market Street from curb to curb and as far as eye could reach in either direction.

Indiana in mauve capes and with the girl cheer-leader attracted much comment. Iowa, red-jacketed, jauntily swings prosaic yardsticks. Kansans march before a Ford bearing appropriate devices, and one boy has a tire hung about his neck. Green smocks brighten this delegation. Nineteen marchers from Maryland carry yellow and black umbrellas. Oklahoma marches in a square made by streamers. Texas, in red and white, sings "The Eyes of Texas Are upon You," a selection most familiar to the Golden Jubilee tour party, whom the Texans trailed through three States on the journey. Utah, a remarkable crowd, uses red and white in its insignia.

Washington Endeavorers are resplendent in green capes and hats. The Tulare County band follows, and then come the Californians. Almost every county has a good-sized delegation, and Los Angeles city and county are represented by a host of marchers. The pages and ushers of the convention in official garb make a picture in themselves.

Then a band from Hip Wo School—a Chinese girls' organization that keeps to a steady beat.

At the city hall, when the marchers had massed their ranks, President Poling referred to the spirit of the city, and in introducing Mayor Angelo J. Rossi mentioned that the visitors would carry away the most pleasant memories of the Golden Jubilee Convention at the Golden Gate. Mayor Rossi declared that this gathering was the most impressive that had been held in San Francisco since he took office.

This Changing World

After a splendid song service introducing the evening service, Otto Nielson, of Texas, delivered a youth address on "Winning World Peace," a clearly stated and soundly argued call to world peace.

Missionaries from a score of countries were presented to the audience that filled every part of the great auditorium, and then came the first of two gripping speeches. It was by Rev. W. A. MacTaggart, of Toronto, Canada, who is president of the Toronto conference of the United Church of Canada, and honorary president of the Canadian Christian Endeavor Union.

CHRISTIANS IN A CHANGING WORLD
From an Address by Rev. W. A. MacTaggart

A great forward movement was taken in Canada six years ago, when we were faced with great difficulties and vexing problems.

We have a large home-missionary territory in Western Canada and in Northern Ontario. We were in the position of unseemly rivalry in these territories where we had, in a small village, a Methodist minister, a Presbyterian minister, and perhaps a Congregational minister —all struggling in little communities where there wasn't a man's job for more than one of them. Each denomination must send in, from mission funds, three hundred dollars, or four hundred, or five hundred, to maintain its own little church. And in the downtown centres of our great cities, where population had been shifting, we needed some kind of inspirational work that the individual denominations seemed powerless to provide.

So we faced the problem frankly and honestly, and I believe wisely.

We said, "It is absurd that we should work separately. It is impossible that we should accomplish as much alone as we might together. Let's join hands and go on unitedly." After long negotiations in the regular way, three church bodies, in June, 1925, joined hands and said, "From this day forward, we shall be one, and we shall do this work together."

We have never been happier in all our lives than we have been since we have worked together as one united church. The only difficulty in our minds at all has been this—"What in the world kept us back so long! What were we waiting for! This should have been done fifty years ago, instead of in 1925!"

Not all the churches joined us. There were congregations that said, "We are happy here. We are satisfied and comfortable. Why should we change? Why should we enter this thing?"

We made our appeal to them about the need of the great prairie provinces and the need of the teaching of the Kingdom of God, by joint efforts, in distant lands. We tried to show the need of economizing in all the places where there was overlapping, so that we would have the more power to apply where the needs are great. Some did not come even then. I think by this time most of these churches are realizing the mistake that was made. We should rise to national conceptions in the church and in the state.

The nations that have made their mark in the last one hundred years are nations that have been united through and through. Suppose the States of the United States had not joined in a common enterprise, even though it meant some sacrifice to all! Where would you be today with several countries—separate like the nations of Europe, seeking selfish causes, throwing up tariff barriers against one another? Where would we have been in Canada if all the provinces were separated—with English-speaking Ontario and French-speaking Quebec side by side? We could have warred with the least provocation. But today we are united; today we are one.

Perhaps you know the story of how we came to be called the *Dominion* of Canada. Sixty-seven years ago, when the various Crown Colonies of Canada were taking steps to unite, there was discussion about a name for the nation. Some wanted to call it the Kingdom of Canada; others would have called it the United Provinces of Canada. But there was no unanimity.

Fortunately there was an elder from New Brunswick in this company, who had formed the good old Christian Endeavor habit of reading the Word of God every morning. In the Seventy-Second Psalm he came one morning on this verse: "He shall have dominion from sea to sea, and from the river to the ends of the earth."

"There it is," he cried. "There Canada has been well described—from ocean to ocean—and from the river into the unknown North! We should call this the Dominion of Canada, *God's dominion!*"

We got from that verse a name. And I believe we got more. I think our Canadian spirit rises above narrow nationalism, and seeks world-wide fellowship. That is the sort of thing we must be for today.

Have you thought of the way in which Jesus Christ rejected narrow nationalism? The people were looking for a Messiah. They thought of a kingdom to come, that would be a Jewish kingdom. A Mussolini would have suited their ambitions. He would have thrust aside their oppressors, freed them from their burdens, and led them into a warfare of supremacy with other peoples. But Jesus was the Messiah. Instead of overlordship, in place of warfare, He presented himself as the Saviour of the world. The Kingdom which He brought was not a Jewish kingdom, nor an earthly one. He called it the Kingdom of God—and it is as wide as the world. Wherever man has trod, wherever there is a living soul that needs the gift of God, there is Jesus with His blessing—and this message, "*He* shall have dominion from sea to sea, and from the river unto the ends of the earth."

The method of Jesus is the only method. The method of peace is the only method.

And if the Christian churches would lead the nations into peace and understanding, they do well to think of union and common effort as a means of spreading that spirit of goodwill and Christian influence. Whatever is narrow and selfish and provincial holds back the advance of His Kingdom.

The second address was by another son of the British Commonwealth, Harry N. Holmes, now of New York. Mr. Holmes was born in Australia and has worked as a Christian leader with the men and young people of four continents. He is a Fellow of the Royal Geographical Society and has received from King George V the Order of the British Empire in connection with his World War work in Flanders. He is field-secretary of the World Alliance for International Friendship through the Churches, and was recently re-elected president of the New York State Christian Endeavor Union.

Portions of his challenging address are quoted below.

A CHANGING WORLD AND ITS NEED

By Harry N. Holmes

Through the centuries, prophets have been haunted by a dream of world brotherhood, to take the place of the actuality of world conflict. That hope of humanity's final oneness runs like a golden thread through history. Even now, in spite of suspicion and hatred, and the clash of nationalism, I say that warlessness remains the spiritual mission of a decent man's thinking.

I am for peace in 1931, because of vivid, unforgettable experiences that came out of France. For I was four and a half years there, and I came away with only two convictions. The first was: I shall never cease to pay my tribute to the men who fought. The second: I would like to do everything in my power, while life remains to me, so that this old world will have its peace conferences *before* it slays ten million boys, instead of *afterward*.

Our world is troubled and confused. The word went along Unter den Linden, in Berlin, "Your banks are gone." Picture the terror clutching thousands who hear, first the rumors, and then the facts, of national disorder and threatened bankruptcy! I think of unemployment; England with one man to every four out of work, and in Lancashire, it is one in every three. I read the literature of gloom and pessimism, picturing a deep abyss yawning before us, through which the nations must pass.

And you and I know that these conditions and these perils, real and imagined, are a part of our account with war. This is all a war debt that has to be paid—not in gold, but in suffering, privation, and tears.

Comradeship Across the Pacific

At San Francisco, we have stood facing the Pacific. It is the biggest thing on the planet—and that appeals to one born in Australia, just as it does to the American. This ocean covers half the surface area of the world. It is the one place where a meridian of longitude goes from pole to pole without touching land. In fact, you could put all the land in the world on the surface area of the Pacific Ocean and still have a strip of water all around the edge. Our race thinks it discovered the Pacific four hundred years ago, and we have banquets to honor Balboa, who crossed the isthmus to see what millions of people had then known for thousands of years!

Around the shores of the Pacific live nearly two-thirds of the people in the world. At its margins are the old land and the new land, the East and the West, spilling over into its blue waters. No wonder one of the last of Roosevelt's messages to youth was this— "The destiny of the United States will be more largely determined by the fact that she faces the Pacific than that she also faces the Atlantic."

The third Mediterranean of history! It is the great challenge. O, comrades of this generation, it is tremendously important to your brother, your boy, my boy, whether the hand that goes across the Pacific Ocean is a clenched fist, or a hand of friendship and understanding.

They quote Kipling like this:

"East is east and west is west,
And never the twain shall meet—"

There they stop. But continue the quotation from this Britisher who understands Asia,

" 'Till two strong men stand face to face,
Though they come from the ends of the earth."

A soul that makes Christianity newly impressive to Western minds today is Eastern—Kagawa, of Japan, a Christian as lofty and as splendid as any in all the world.

One thing we must do. on the shores of the Pacific, that we have been doing along the boundary line to the north. There it is—a thousand miles of mountain, then a thousand miles of prairie, then a thousand miles of lake, and a thousand miles of river. No fort, no gun, no soldier anywhere across that great expanse—and security and peace are safer because they are not there!

The other pacific task is not political. What we must do beyond that is in the realm of the spirit. Christian Endeavor, in sixty countries, helps in that task of establishing world brotherhood through world religion.

Christian Endeavorers have holiday homes all up and down the English coast. A German boy was invited. He expected to stay three days. Instead, as he told us in Berlin last summer, he stayed three weeks. When he was leaving he said to his hosts, "Good bye. I cannot agree with you in my mind, but I can in my heart. My heart has conquered my mind."

When the heart is all right with the power of God and the love of brotherhood. there is nothing worth fighting about that you can not settle by reason. That is the purpose of the World Court, in which America should now take her place. The World Court is an American child. Every American reservation has been met. We should throw the weight of our moral influence into this peaceful method for settling differences. The disarmament conference is coming—inevitable because the World Court is succeeding.

The Peace Pact of Paris, outlawing war in the life of nations, was ratified by sixty nations. Yet with the Peace Pact signed, thirty million men in the world are in armies. Seventy per cent more men under arms now than in 1913! No wonder the President has said, "The first task to help the world recover is to cut off some of that expenditure." We disarmed Germany, and we pledged our word to follow her example. Now the conference is called—sixty nations, two thousand delegates, to be presided over by a great Christian statesman, Mr. Arthur Henderson.

Will there be more war debts, more lives sacrificed to greed and impatience, more destruction and disaster? Will the Pacific Ocean some day echo with the boom of cannons and the conflict of many nations? Not if Christ has His way with us. Not if we are loyal to Him, in word and in life. Christian Endeavorers and all Christian young people may well enlist in the greatest of all international goals —making peace secure, maintaining brotherhood, defeating selfish nationalism.

Mr. Holmes then presented for signature Youth's Disarmament Petition, printed on cards which were circulated throughout the great audience. Thousands of these were signed at the auditorium and many others were turned in later, when the delegates had fully considered this action. Here at San Francisco a new expression of Christian youth on the world's disarmament opportunity was launched.

Youth's Disarmament Petition

To the President of the United States:

Believing that the coming International Disarmament Conference, to be held next year, presents one of the supreme opportunities of the present generation to further the cause of international good will and peace,—

WE, young citizens of the United States, respectfully call upon our government to take leadership with a definite program for the reduction of armaments.

The Peace Pact of Paris, ratified by fifty-eight nations, renounced war as an instrument of national policy, and agreed to settle all controversies by pacific means. We firmly believe that this great forward step in international understanding absolutely implies a very substantial curtailment of the armed forces of the nations.

We believe that our own patriotism in this enlightened generation can best be exemplified by aiding our country to live in the highest spirit of concord and good will with all other countries.

"National honor" in all lands now points to the signed pledges of the Peace Pact of Paris, rather than to excessive and selfish nationalism.

C. Y. CHENG, LL. D.
*Moderator of the United Church of
Christ of China*

CHAPTER VI

FRIENDSHIP AND HARMONY
Wednesday, July 15

Youth for War or Peace?—An Inter-Racial Musical Program—Dr. Cory Speaks on Making a "Triumphant Harmony" of Life

WEDNESDAY in the convention week might be called "harmony day." The theme of the morning session was friendship and good will, and the evening meeting was given almost entirely to music, with an able address on harmony in life, by Dr. A. E. Cory, of Indianapolis.

The day began with the faculty breakfast at the Hotel William Taylor, followed by another of the splendid series of Quiet Hour services, with the message, "An Old Fashioned Hill (Matthew 27:33)," brought by Vice-President Foulkes. "International Good Will and World Peace" was the theme of the first-period conferences (sixteen in number), followed by the continuing series of methods conferences on fifteen subjects, comprising twenty-five separate sessions.

In the mass meeting that followed, Dr. Poling told of the partial destruction by fire, in February, of Williston Church, Portland, Me., the birthplace of Christian Endeavor. A memorial window made possible through the generosity of Mrs. Clark, will be placed in the church when rebuilt. "All friends of Christian Endeavor may become contributors to this worthy memorial," Dr. Poling said. "The Financial Secretary of the International Society, Mr. Wright, will be glad to receive your gifts."

Honor Unions

Banners for the financial support of the International Christian Endeavor movement were given to Virginia, Mexico, and Wisconsin Unions.

In the subscription-registration campaign conducted by C. C. Hamilton, publication-manager of THE CHRISTIAN ENDEAVOR WORLD, banners were won by Wisconsin, Pennsylvania, New Jersey, and Arizona, the first four State unions to reach their quotas. These States led the parade.

The States were divided into five groups in this campaign, and a friendly rivalry has been promoted within each group of States. The first three in each group to attain their subscription goals received special recognition banners. These were as follows:

Group A, Pennsylvania, California, and New York.

Group B. Illinois, New Jersey, and Kansas.

Group C, Washington, Maryland, and Indiana.

Group D. Wisconsin only attained her goal.

Group E. Arizona only attained her goal.

The highest honors go to the two unions credited with fifty or more registrations and subscriptions. The Eastern District of Wisconsin (John Hoffman, Union representative), and Philadelphia County in Pennsylvania (Violet Keiser, Union representative), so qualified.

Unions whose CHRISTIAN ENDEAVOR WORLD representatives are credited with twenty-five or more San Francisco Convention registrations and twenty-five or more WORLD subscriptions are the following:

Brooklyn, New York State, Miss Lucy Weber, representative.

Denver, Colorado, Miss Lois Knapp and Edward DeHaven, representatives.

Milwaukee, Wisconsin, Mrs. Alta Alexander, representative.

Salt Lake City, Utah, Hewes Robertson, representative.

Banner unions, credited with fifteen subscriptions and fifteen registrations are: Three G District, Arizona; Lehigh County, Pennsylvania; Stanislaus-Merced District, California; Northampton County, Pennsylvania.

Followed then a stirring address by Rev. Walter W. Van Kirk, of New York, associate secretary of the Federal Council of the Churches of Christ in America. Mr. Van Kirk is not only an informed and eloquent speaker, but his words come with convicting power.

YOUTH FOR WAR OR PEACE?

Portions of an Address by Rev. Walter W. Van Kirk

There are many who care nothing for either war or peace. There are young men on the streets of our cities who are utterly indifferent. Yet there is a constructive minority of young people that is deeply interested. A small group—but it is always the small group that transform the world. Jesus, a carpenter from Nazareth, with a small band of followers, overthrew the Roman Empire.

Youth must realize that the war system is deep-rooted and will not be destroyed merely by passing resolutions. Young people must learn the facts and be able to present them. Why do men fight? What do they get out of war? Young Britons went to war to save their country. But all they got out of it is to be allowed to walk the streets of London or Birmingham, idle and useless. For war is absolutely futile. It never succeeds.

The biggest problem before the world today is that of disarmament Last year the nations of the world spent five billions of dollars on armament, and America spent one billion of these five.

Youth is convinced increasingly that the attainment of peace can only be had through the removal of all forms of social, racial, and industrial inequality. That is why many of our American high-school and college students are interesting themselves in the great social, economic, and political problems of the present day. These young people want to see their own government taking a more active and constructive part in the affairs of the world—in the strengthening of the World Court and in the functioning of the League of Nations.

The young people of today are world-minded. They do not believe in the political theory of isolation. They are gratified that President Hoover has taken the initiative, through his proposal for a year's war-debt and reparations moratorium, of helping in the economic reconstruction of Germany and other nations. Many of these young people are convinced that no nation can maintain a position of economic independence. They are sceptical of high tariff walls and of other economic barriers that tend to keep the nations apart.

"They Want to Live"

Young people are opposed to the war system of the nations because they want to live. They want to live not because they are "yellow" nor because they are afraid to die. They want to live in order to give form and substance to their dreams for a better and a happier world. They want to build homes and see children blossom into maturity. They are all the more anxious to live because they know that death upon the battlefield accomplishes nothing, as wars are fought today. Life must not be forfeited for no apparent good. Young people have come to the conclusion that the younger generation has been used for cannon fodder long enough. They are sick and tired of rifle-bearing and bayonet-plunging. Because they are afraid? Not for a minute!

The more forward of our young people have repudiated the military philosophy of life because they see stretching out before them a better way, a way of peace and understanding.

Youth wants a part in the remaking of the world. Youth has earned that right and means to have it!

The third of the four daily Youth Radio Conferences followed, with Harold Singer presiding and Dr. Poling as speaker. The theme was: "Youth and a Warless World." As before, Dr. Poling answered a number of questions from delegates.

At 1.15, two important luncheons were held. Pastors met at the William Taylor Hotel, with Dr. Poling and Dr. MacTaggart as speakers. Rev. Harry Thomas Stock and Stanley B. Vandersall spoke at the college luncheon ("for all present, former, and future college students"), which was held at the Whitcomb Hotel on Market Street.

The recreation and sightseeing features of this convention have been superb. Visitors by the thousand have been enthused in the wide variety of scenery opened to them by the many trips by bus, train, and electric car, that have been provided in the San Francisco area. The Wednesday afternoon sightseeing opportunity, a steamer ride on San Francisco Bay, passing the Golden Gate and with splendid views of the Bay Cities and nearby mountains, surpassed all the others.

At 5.30, seven hundred persons gathered at the Whitcomb Hotel for the official convention banquet, which honored Mrs. Francis E. Clark and other distinguished Alumni. This event is reported in more detail in Chapter X.

Musical Hours

While the official banquet in honor of Mrs. Francis E. Clark was being held in Hotel Whitcomb, Song-leader Homer Rodeheaver was busy in the Convention Auditorium in one of his inimitable song services.

Much of the popularity of Mr. Rodeheaver lies in the fact that he not only gets people to sing, but that he varies the procedure, introducing solos, quartettes, singing antiphonally, and so forth, all exceedingly interesting and sometimes surprising. In this convention he was splendidly supported by a magnificent chorus of 350 voices. How they could sing!

But the immense auditorium is filled by this time, and the worship period has begun. Prayer was offered by Rev. Newton E. Moats, of San Francisco.

Even in the musical part this convention was inter-racial. The First African Methodist Episcopal choir of Oakland sang beautifully a number of Negro spirituals, as only Negroes can sing them. And now we learned that Mr. Rodeheaver comes from the South, from Tennessee, to be exact. And he knew something about spirituals. He said that these songs are universal, common to the plantations of Tennessee, Alabama, and other States. To prove it, he started a spiritual without telling what it was to be; but the Negro choir joined in before he had finished the first line.

Then came the Hawaiian group, gayly garbed and garlanded. Two Chinese girls who were to sing a duet got the giggles, and delighted the audience with their youthful gayety. A Spanish Hawaiian sang in Spanish and English with fine effect.

Mr. Rodeheaver sang "Draw Near, All Ye People," from "Elijah," the choir joining in chorus parts.

Those that heard the next address will not soon forget it. This was the message of Dr. A. E. Cory, of Indianapolis, director of the board of pensions of the Disciples of Christ, on "A World Call."

HARMONY IN LIFE

By Dr. A. E. Cory

The world can have the triumphant harmony of a great symphony, or it can have the discordant and harsh voices of discord. The world voices may be so scattered and widely separated that there is no volume or unison. As one listens to a great chorus, he can not help imagining the singers scattered down the main street of the world singing alone, each one making his own song and not thinking of the others. The world was like that when a man walked by a quiet lake in centuries gone. He looked upon every man and every nation and said, "There is a place for you."

You may be sounding a high note, or your voice may reach the depths. I call you to sing not alone, but to join in that chorus which the Father desires in which "all God's children" shall have a part.

Here and there men are joining in a united song, but the world call of Christ is for us to make an anthem of praise in which every voice of the world shall share.

A Task for Every One

The Christian must live the Jesus life. He must carry it to others. The evangelization of the world must be reached by building the kingdom of God by patient, constructive processes. Every follower of Christ must not only believe, but have the conviction of the world's need of Christ. The world is composed not only of geographical areas of life. The oratorio of God includes every human group.

We must recognize every man who is a worshipper. Wherever there is truth in his religion, we must seek fellowship with him, and take Christ to him, recognizing that truth as far as it goes.

When men in far-away lands lift up their voices in praise of our Lord, let us not seek to make that church of the Orient Western, but let it be Christ's.

The life that we live will give to the world its life. If our lives are secular, we shall take a secular Christ to the world. Three great forces are contending today. Their voices of necessity can not be in harmony. Communism, with its godless and class philosophy; nationalism, which seeks good for one race and one blood; and the gospel of the living Christ, which gives life to every class and to every race.

Other religions are decaying. God is putting upon us the tremendous task of keeping religion alive in the world. The task of bringing the world to Christ is just beginning. Any religion that "digs in" dies. It is the religion that is on the march that lives.

The world cannot live without Christ, but we must take to the world a risen, living Christ. If our lives are dead and cold, and we take a dead Christ to the world, we shall not down the world. But if our lives live in Him, we shall take a living Lord who will bring harmony to the voices of men.

Comrades of the Jubilee

Small touches in this meeting were the presentation of a bouquet of gladioli to Mrs. Clark from the Marin County union. Also the Intermediates of Maryland sent fifty dollars to help the work of Christian Endeavor. Dr. Poling called on the audience as "Comrades of the Jubilee" to make contributions for the world-wide program of the movement. Mrs. Clark sat in front, and those that responded to Dr. Poling's appeal—and they were many—marched past her, and placed their gifts in a basket which she held.

A resolution was passed pledging Christian Endeavor to the missionary tasks of the church.

Another delightful feature was the playing of a violin choir of more than fifteen, which rendered several selections with excellent taste and full-toned harmony.

Mr. Rodeheaver stated that it was planned to sing the favorite song of each decade since 1881. The first selected for the year 1891 was "The Child of a King," which was finely rendered by the four Higgins sisters. This was the first song Dr. Poling remembers hearing his mother sing.

The song for 1901 was "The Glory Song," written by Mr. Gabriel. That for 1911 was "The Way of the Cross Leads Home." The 1921 song was "Safe in the Arms of Jesus," and the song for the next decade, ending 1931, was the convention song, "Greater Things than These."

A Chinese choir from San Francisco and Oakland Presbyterian churches gave the convention a real thrill with their beautiful singing. Kipling's "Recessional" was rendered in English, and "Brighten the Corner," in Chinese.

More Negro spirituals followed, "What kind of shoes you goin' to wear?" and so on down a list of the glories of heaven. "Little David, play on your harp" was enjoyed immensely.

Rev. A. J. Ungersma from Washington rendered some fine music on a piano-accordion, and then the choir sang the "Hallelujah Chorus" as a climax to a wonderful day.

In the afternoon of Wednesday, the Dixie States and the California Christian Endeavor Union held conventions, receiving encouraging reports and outlining plans for future work.

A FEW NEW YORK STATE DELEGATES AT THE JUBILEE
CONVENTION IN SAN FRANCISCO

CARLTON M. SHERWOOD

Elected General Secretary of the International Society of Christian Endeavor at the Golden Jubilee International Christian Endeavor Convention in San Francisco

CHAPTER VII

THE LAST DAY OF THE FEAST
Thursday, July 16

President Hoover Speaks—A Splendid Interpretation of
Gandhi by Dr. Fred B. Fisher—Carlton M. Sherwood
Becomes General Secretary—A Concluding
Service of Rare Power and Spirituality

IN this concluding morning of the Golden Jubilee Convention,
the faculty took counsel together for the last time around
the breakfast tables in the William Taylor Hotel. The Quiet
Hour service was splendidly attended, and Dr. William Hiram
Foulkes gave the fourth of his inspiring "Mountain Top Talks,"
using the theme "The Mountain in Galilee" (Matthew 28:16).

The theme in the first period forum sessions was "The Gospel with a United Church around the World." The final group
of simultaneous methods conferences, using the theme, "Trained
and Loyal Youth . . . for Christ and the Church," brought
to a close the practical and inspiring "school of the convention." More about the significant conference program of the
convention is included in Chapter X.

President Hoover Speaks

The conference periods were shortened by a few minutes
so that the delegates could be in their places in the main auditorium at 11.05 o'clock.

Dr. Poling presided at this historic service. The thousands
who attended will long remember the minute of absolute quite
that ensued as the official chronometer approached the 11.15
markings. Then clear as a bell came the introductory remarks
of a radio announcer at the eastern rim of the country, who said
that the President of the United States would speak from the
cabinet-room of the White House, in Washington, to be broadcast through the entire network of the National Broadcasting
Company.

Not a word of the splendid address that followed was lost.
The President's voice came to the delegates through the ampli-

fying system that had been used in all the main sessions of the convention. It was as if the speaker stood beside Dr. Poling at the platform desk.

The President's happy references to the movement and its anniversary, to its founder Dr. Clark whose helpmate sat among the group on the platform, and to the world-wide implications of Christian Endeavorer's ministry could not be cheered. But even the silence of the delegates was eloquent with approval and respect. When the address was completed, the delegates joined in the singing of the Doxology. It had been indeed a rare witness to the unseen powers of the Almighty that a former Junior Endeavorer in Oregon, now called to high office, could send his greetings across the continent with the speed of light, while other waiting millions listened in.

The President's message to the convention, and to all Endeavorers, has been printed in one of the forward pages of this report. It deserves to be preserved in the Christian archives of America, as the Chief Executive's splendid testimony to the usefulness of religion in citizenship and to his personal loyalty to the ideals of his own youth.

Youth and the Old Gospel

C. C. Hamilton presided during the next period when Rev. Louis H. Evans, of Pomona, Cal., spoke on "Youth and the Old Gospel."

"A difficult subject," he said, "for even old folks look with aversion on anything that is aged. All that is old is not useless, although some of it is. We must always be ready to let go what has served its purpose. That is the price of progress. But progress is not always destruction. Sometimes it is conservation. There are some things that you and I never can give up, because they are everlastingly true. That two plus two equal four will always be true no matter what happens in the world. And that is true of Christianity. 'Heaven and earth shall pass away, but my word shall never pass away.' Are you and I willing to hold to anything that is 2,000 years old? I believe we are. While history changes, the human heart does not change.

"A rich young ruler came to Jesus asking what he must do to inherit everlasting life. Here was youth—hungry. Looking for satisfaction. So long as the gospel satisfies it will never be old. It gives us peace and pardon. Property is not the big problem today. The big problem is sin. And there is no solution of the sin problem but Christ."

The speaker pointed to India's holy men tormenting the body, but torture did not bring them peace. Nor can science remove the stain of sin from the heart. Lady Macbeth was taken as an example of an awakened conscience which tried in vain to wipe off the blood of murder from her white hands. Only the blood of Christ can do that; and therefore the gospel never can be old.

Mr. Evans told of seeing sweeper people, one of the lower castes of India, singing with joy, "At the cross, at the cross, where I first saw the light, the burden of my sin rolled away." They had made a great discovery and felt themselves heirs of the ages. Man is made for the ages and nothing less can satisfy him. Science cannot measure beyond the grave. Only Jesus Christ can. The gospel will never be old because we shall always need Jesus and He can satisfy the heart.

He pointed out that we have lots of ideals, but what we need is power to live up to them. We need the old gospel and the old family altar to prevent the destruction of many of our homes.

"Let us go back home," concluded the speaker, "with the thought, 'Jesus shall reign.' He cannot fail. An Oriental was asked, 'Who is the man of tomorrow?' and he answered, 'Jesus is the man of tomorrow.'"

Gandhi and the New India

The great audience was held enthralled by Dr. Fred B. Fisher, of Ann Arbor, Mich., former Methodist missionary bishop in India, as he spoke on Mahatma Gandhi and the New India. No words can express the fervor of this great speech, simple, direct, heart-searching, and filled with tremendous moral passion. The following is quite inadequate, yet it may give a faint idea of a speech that abounded in good things.

We are interested in Gandhi, he began, because he is the incarnation of the greatest idea the world has ever had—the ideal of peace. We of the West have little right to speak about peace. We have always been men of war from the very dawn of history. Today two-thirds of the population of the world are under European control. We have the spirit of conquerors. To conquer we have made all sorts of sacrifices.

Perhaps, he continued, I ought not to talk about sacrifice. We have never sacrificed anything. We have grabbed everything in sight.

Dr. Fisher is a friend of Gandhi. He told how one day Gandhi turned Dr. Fisher's head toward his wife and said: "Look at his profile. Look at that chin. Imagine a man with a chin like that talking about peace!" Gandhi has made the world self-conscious on the matter of militarism and peace. Browning once said, "One solitary great man is worth the world." A great physician said that some day we shall be able to inject germs of health into diseased bodies and cure disease. Great men are these germs of health that transform the world.

Gandhi has power. He has more power than any other man ever had. Three hundred million men and women revere him. He is their flag, their all.

Very vividly Dr. Fisher presented to us an idea of what three hundred million people mean. It would take all the people of the Philippine and Hawaiian islands, Canada, Labrador, Mexico, the five republics of Central America, South America, the islands of the Atlantic, England, Ireland, Scotland, Wales, Belgium, France, and Spain, and yet you would not have made up your three hundred millions. More people die in India of starvation every year than live in Belgium. That is Gandhi's following.

Gandhi incarnates the life of Christ and makes it practical. He does not use the Christian name. He speaks no party shibboleth, but he lives the Sermon on the Mount.

We shall never bring about a warless world by words spoken in Geneva or elsewhere. It has first to be incarnated in men. Pacifists cannot do it. Only strong-willed fighting men ready to die for peace can do it.

Jesus did not ask us to kill our personalities, but make them greater, lift them to higher levels.

Dr. Fisher gave us an intimate description of Gandhi, a small man, insignificant in appearance, voice resonant, eyes deep-set, piercing, intelligent, passionate. One of the great principles of his life he calls *Ahimsa*, harmlessness, or better still: "I will not kill, I will not cripple, any living thing in order to benefit my own life." Gandhi got his first lesson in "harmlessness" when he was a boy. Sitting one day in a room with his mother he saw a scorpion, a deadly animal, on his mother's foot. He was terrified and cried out that there was a scorpion on her foot. She said, "Hush-sh-sh, which foot is it?" never moving. "The right foot," said the boy. Slowly, without moving the foot the mother took off her silk shawl, dropped it over the scorpion, lifted it, and then shook it quietly out of the folds of the shawl. She then told him that animals will not hurt if we are not afraid of them and do them no harm. *Ahimsa!* Harmlessness!

Dr. Fisher then launched into a description of the horrors of war, telling incidents the like of which we must never forget. With great passion, because of these things, he cried, "I'm against it. I'm against it."

With telling effect he described a young Indian's finding, lying against a tottering post used to hold up barbed wire, an image of the Christ. The Indian rapped it and it sounded hollow. "See," he cried passionately, "Your Christ is hollow, hollow." Then, "O God help me to be both an Indian and a Christian." This man today is Gandhi's most trusted lieutenant.

Carl Sandburg stood before a newspaper office during the war and watched a young man move buttons to mark the western front. But no one thought that to move these buttons ten thousand young men were wallowing on their bellies in the mud, and those boys *died* to move the buttons. We must never forget the ghastly realities of war, and we must not let youth forget them either.

Gandhi has a different principle and method. And he won his fight with England without the loss of a single life. He believes in force, but not material force. Spiritual, which is both higher and more difficult. It is the method of Jesus. For Jesus on the cross is the highest incarnation of the *Ahimsa* dream.

India has another principle, *Satyagraha*, "silence, never violence, but insistence on truth." In ancient times in India, for punishment men were sometimes trussed in straw rope, tied to the tail of wild bulls, and the bulls were driven through the streets to the desert, the man being banged and smashed against the walls of the narrow streets. When at last the fury of the bull was spent friends of the man would pick him up and take off the straw. When he recovered consciousness he would say, "*Satyagraha*, I still believe."

This is the spirit in which Gandhi believes and which he manifests. *Harmlessness, non-violence, spiritual force against swords and guns; and Gandhi has won.*

Final Sightseeing Opportunities

The delegates said their farewells to the convention city of wind and sunshine in the Thursday afternoon hours that were provided for recreation. A number of the delegates had not had the privilege of all the sightseeing journeys, for the number of reservations that could be accepted was limited. Good friends in the churches of San Francisco made their cars available on this final afternoon of the convention period, so that hundreds more could be taken through historic and picturesque and progressive San Francisco and to Golden Gate Park, the Golden Gate itself, the Presidio, the Fishermen's Wharf, Telegraph Hill, and other world-famous places.

Consecration and Reconsecration

For days we have been climbing, climbing, and now on Thursday evening we have reached the mountain top in this closing meeting of the convention. After the praise service, led by Homer Rodeheaver, comes an address by Harold Graham, Hollywood, youth speaker, whose topic is "Youth and Christian Missions," or as he rephrased it, "New Feet on Old Paths." There is but one hope for missions, he said—Youth. There is but one missionary word of Christ—*Go*. This thought he developed in glowing language that won the heart.

Then a greeting from Rev. Wallace J. Anderson, president of the Korean Christian Endeavor Union. Many Korean Christians, he said, have given up some other religion to become Christians, and they are sometimes disappointed because the church does not give them what they expected, since they judge the church by Christ, its Master. He told of what Christian Endeavor is doing to teach and train these people.

Introductions

It is time for introductions. There are the pianists and organist, whose services have been wonderful. Mr. Sherwood introduces Bert H. Davis, publicity director, and is himself "introduced" by Fred D. Parr, associate chairman of the convention. Paul Shoup, chairman, who has come 400 miles to attend this session, receives an ovation. Miss Mildreth Haggard, Junior leader of the convention, is hailed tumultuously, and deservedly.

Then Mrs. Francis E. Clark receives a jewelled Christian Endeavor pin, which greatly pleases the audience.

New trustees are chosen—the list appears in another section of this book.

New General Secretary

Now comes an event of the convention—the choice of a new general secretary for the International Society of Christian Endeavor. The trustees' choice is Mr. Carlton M. Sherwood, whom the great audience accepted with acclaim, to follow, as Dr. Poling said, in the noble succession of John Willis Baer and William Shaw and their associates. Dr. Poling continued:

Trained in our movement and captured by the genius of its spirit and plan, Carlton M. Sherwood brings to its executive guidance a veritable wealth of experience and achievement. His sterling leadership in New York State and in the prohibition and Christian citizenship activities of the country have already made him of national reputation. He is eloquent, dynamic, tireless, statesmanlike, and consecrated—single-eyed in his devotion to this cause. My heart is filled with gratitude as he accepts our high commission.

Carlton M. Sherwood becomes the field marshal of a new advance. "Trusting in the Lord Jesus Christ for strength," he will lead us into "Greater Things than These."

Hundreds of thousands of Christian Endeavorers will receive this announcement with joy, and join me in the prayer, "God bless our General Secretary."

Mr. Sherwood feelingly responded, accepting the high trust placed upon him. His formal induction into office was participated in by both Dr. Poling and Mrs. Francis E. Clark. When the new leader bent to receive Mrs. Clark's kiss, the crowd rejoiced and applauded.

General Secretary Sherwood regards Christian Endeavor as

one of the greatest forces in his life. He was a member as a boy, and was not far past eighteen when the Buffalo, N. Y., Christian Endeavor Union chose him for its president—their youngest executive to that time. Later he was a vice-president of the New York State Christian Endeavor Union and also Life Work Recruit Superintendent. Mr. Sherwood served actively in the World War on three fronts, and at the signing of the armistice, in 1918, entered Y. M. C. A. work with the army, and was in charge of religious work at Flag Hut, Brest, France, for a number of months. On returning to the United States, he was chosen general secretary of the New York State Christian Endeavor Union.

In the intervening years, he has been extension secretary of the International Society of Christian Endeavor, editor of THE CHRISTIAN ENDEAVOR WORLD, and executive secretary of the National Citizens Committee of One Thousand, a movement for law observance and enforcement.

Mr. Sherwood has spoken on religious topics, on world peace, and on prohibition in almost every State of the Union and in the leading cities of Canada and to other groups overseas. As editor and writer, he has contributed almost continuously to religious journalism for a number of years. His abilities in administration and program-building have been widely recognized.

To echo President Poling's words, "God bless our General Secretary."

Dr. Fisher's Consecration Message

Dr. Fred B. Fisher, former Methodist bishop in India, now pastor of a great church in the University of Michigan centre, Ann Arbor, had thrilled delegates in a daytime address on Gandhi. Now, as the convention approaches its inspiring close, he is heard in a short, simply-constructed sermon of power and beauty that sums up the spirit of all the great convention messages. Dr. Fisher is speaking of Christian conduct, in personal and practical terms. He holds Jesus Christ before us as perfect example and His cross as the centre of His power. "Do you accept the cross?" he asks. "Take its weight upon you. That is the way to life."

PRINCIPLES FOR CHRISTIAN POWER
From an Address by Dr. Fred B. Fisher

I follow the first great humanist. Such a humanist as He was, I would strive to be.

There are four enemies to human welfare. The first is poverty. In this country you do not know poverty. I have seen bent, starving old women pick grains of wheat from the offal of beasts in India. The very animals are not so helpless as many millions of people in the world today, who lack food and the means to get it. Nations went into the World War in 1914 to defend the neutrality and national life of tiny Belgium, with 8,000,000 citizens. There are 7,500,000 deaths in India every year from starvation and malnutrition, but nobody thinks much about this, because these people have brown skins.

The second enemy of the people is ignorance. I will not speak of illiteracy. The judgment to move forward free from superstition is worth more than mere ability to read and to write. The world is fettered today by its superstitions.

Disease is the third enemy. Here scientists must step in. The church does well to give science every means and power to cure disease in large-scale terms. Whole nations must be treated to make them immune.

It is violence that is the fourth enemy. All four could be summed up in sin. Violence is the biggest sin in modern life. The sin of one selfish man against another. The sin of a great corporation against the rights of others. The sin of one race against other weaker races. It is hatred that organizes competition. We have never organized love. Co-operation is the lesson we have never wanted to learn.

Let's have a flag of love, to which all can swear loyalty. Men will march beneath such a flag, while they tire of the banners that carry violence in their folds.

I myself have to choose what inspires me in life, what integrates my spirit, and to reject what confuses and destroys.

The gospel of my life, as I express it in words, is this:

Four Forms of Christian Power

First, no one can offend me. I carry away no hatred. I do not yield; but, when I stand firm, I do it without rancor or offence. Such poise as I have comes from Jesus Christ. We must begin world peace in our own lives, with the principle, "No one can offend me."

Second, I can not be discouraged. Because every new situation carries its own springs of encouragement. In the darkest hour hope is found, and in the deepest springs. I can not be discouraged.

Third, I will let others think, and continue to love them. Voltaire said to his opponent, his neighbor, "I don't believe one word you say, but I would give my right hand to defend your right to say it."

Fourth, Jesus Christ is my perfect example. The more you bear a cross, the better it becomes. Thank God for science, but thank God more, a thousand times more, for the power of the cross. Will you rejoice in the cross? I promise you greatness, a great life. Let's go along together, young America. Let's prove each for himself that these four principles express what a Christian today must believe and must do. Do you accept the cross? Take its weight upon you. That is the way to life.

Before the Benediction

The Golden Jubilee Convention nears its close. What will it mean in my life? "You will never be the same again," declares Dr. Poling. "Some things you planned will never be done, because you desert them. Some hopes fondly held will be presently surrendered. We may become ministers of life. We shall, many of us, be wholly changed."

Choices for an advance in Christian life were proposed. Some would become full-time workers in the Master's vineyards, fully surrendering all of life to Him. Dr. Poling made such a decision hard. "Do not stand as one who says, 'I will live entirely for Him' if you find it easy to do so," he counselled. "It should be a hard choice, not made without consulting qualified adult advisers who know you well." More than fifty young people, young men and young women of fine, courageous, outstanding types, not only stood in their places, but came to the platform.

Thousands stood in the call for those who would give themselves in part-time Christian service. A large number, many hundreds, declared themselves tithers. A few confessed Christ for the first time as Saviour, although it was evident from the type of gathering that almost all those present were declared Christians and were active in church and society work.

When the main session, swept by this spirit of surrender and worship, had been brought to a close, Dr. Poling summoned those who had made these choices, and other friends, to an after-meeting in an adjoining hall.

No sweeter moments in all the convention than these. Golden minutes of the Golden Jubilee. Truly the spirit of this prayer meeting, in a large hall close to the Pacific, was akin to the spirit of that first meeting, now commemorated, when for the first time a group of young people in distant New England spoke that phrase of power and purpose, "Trusting in the Lord Jesus Christ for strength, I will."

BERT H. DAVIS,
of Utica, New York, in charge of newspaper publicity for the convention.

WILLIAM UNMACK
Executive Secretary, Convention Committee

CHAPTER VIII

YOUNG PEOPLE'S RADIO CONFERENCES

Dr. Poling Broadcast at Four Noon Meetings During the Convention—An Address and a Question-and-Answer Period Presented through KPO

ON four days, beginning Monday, July 13, Dr. Daniel A. Poling broadcast a talk and his answers to a number of delegates' queries, using the facilities of Radio Station KPO. The broadcast was a noon feature of the convention program for three days of the four. On Tuesday, because the morning session was adjourned early due to. parade preparations, Dr. Poling spoke from the radio studio. KPO is a station of the National Broadcasting Company, through whose system Dr. Poling has spoken each Sunday afternoon, in the program of the Youth Radio Conference. The same station and company co-operated in the broadcasting of President Hoover's Thursday morning message.

Monday's Program

In the first of his four radio addresses, Dr. Poling spoke ten minutes on "Youth and Christ." Dr. Paul C Brown, Pacific Coast secretary of the International Society, presided.

YOUTH AND CHRIST

From an Address by Dr. Daniel A. Poling

I am frequently asked the question: "Are young people as religious today as formerly? Are they interested in religion?" I shall be surprised if I escape that question in this convention. (In fact, it was one of the first questions submitted by delegates of the Golden Jubilee Convention.)

I tell you today, out of my fairly wide and comprehensive experience, that I have never known the time when young people of all groups and classes and ages and conditions responded more quickly to the appeal of religion, and specifically to the challenge of the Lord Jesus Christ, than now.

This convention is one demonstration of that fact.

Four years ago, in this month, I stood looking down at a parade that swept through the streets of Cleveland, Ohio. By my side was one of the most brilliant newspaper men of the United States. More than twenty thousand young people were marching, under flags and accompanied by floats and bands, on that day in Cleveland. This man turned to me, and with surprise reflected on his face, said: "What is it? What does it all mean? What is your explanation?"

I replied, "Well, it isn't a prize fight. It isn't a great athletic exhibition . ." although our young people are vitally interested in athletics. I am happy to discover that the fastest human of them all, Wycoff, is one of our Christian Endeavorers. "These young people," I said, "have not come to Cleveland pleasure-bent. This is a Christian Endeavor convention. These are young Christians from the four corners of the continent, and from the far places of the earth, who would be about their Master's business. They are studying now to show themselves approved unto God in order that they may become unashamed to work."

Yes, if my experience teaches me anything or justifies any statement at all, it teaches me that young people are incurably religious; it justifies my saying that the program of the Christ reaches youth. The program of the Christ with reference to the building of a constructive peace. The program of the Christ with regard to prohibition and law enforcement. That program of the Christ, in pre-eminently winning young men and young women to Him for all His plans, in changing their lives, in regenerating their hearts, is before them, when it is given adequate voice, when we ourselves are true to it.

Long ago a young lawyer came to Jesus. I am sure he had been in contact with the Master many times. On the occasion to which I refer, this young lawyer said, "I will follow, Thee; I will follow Thee whithersoever Thou goest." And the Master looked upon him and replied, essentially in these words, "I wonder if you understand. I am glad to have your declaration. The foxes have their holes, the birds of the air have their nests, but the Son of Man hath no pillow for His head."

Do you think that the man who spoke first turned away then? That he declined the suggestion? That he refused the implications of hardship and suffering? No! I am glad to believe that he went forward, and followed through.

Why do I say that? I say it because, as I know young people, I never find them turning away from the Christian program because they have been invited to open their veins and shed their blood. Again and again I find them creeping from their spiritual cradles and going out to the ends of the world to make their lives count.

I can not refrain today from referring again to my old friend, Tom Hannay, of this State, who was the associate of Paul Brown years ago. I saw him last in 1913 at the Los Angeles International Christian Endeavor Convention. I had learned to love him. He was a manly fellow, a splendid specimen physically, and a radiant personality. One night, after a session, we walked in the streets of Los Angeles, and he told me of his determination to be a missionary in Africa.

I sought to dissuade him. I pled the case for the United States and for the Pacific Coast, and told him that it seemed to me his duty was here. He smiled, smiled his contagious smile, and reaffirmed his determination. He went to Africa. He did not stay there long. The jungle fever caught him, laid him low, and he passed.

For years, I have kept about me, generally on my desk, his last words: "Finally, my friend, I would leave you face to face with Jesus Christ." That was his message. He caught it from the face of Jesus Christ.

That is the message of this Christian Endeavor convention. It is essentially through all departments and in all activities the message of the Christian Endeavor movement. My friend, I would leave you, everywhere, at all times, face to face with Jesus Christ.

After a closing prayer, Dr. Poling answered many questions that had been turned in by delegates, following advance announcements of Saturday and Sunday. These were read by Chairman Brown. A number of the questions answered in this and the following periods are quoted in the concluding pages of this chapter.

On Christian Citizenship

Speaking at the studio of KPO on Tuesday noon, shortly before the convention parade, Dr. Poling repeated a portion of the Christian citizenship message that was included in the Saturday evening keynote address. This was particularly significant in advance of Christian Endeavor's demonstrations of the strength and vigor of Christian youth, given new meaning in the parade of thousands of the crusading forces in downtown San Francisco.

W. Roy Breg, Southern secretary of the International Society, introduced Dr. Poling and read to him an even dozen of questions, ranging from an inquiry about Christian Endeavor in the Episcopal churches to one dealing with Niagara Falls. Several of these questions are quoted in succeeding pages.

A Warless World

Wednesday's radio conference, like Monday's, was a part of the Golden Jubilee Convention program, with a splendid attendance of young people. Harold Singer, Mid-West Secretary of the International Society, presided.

YOUTH AND A WARLESS WORLD
From an Address by Dr. Daniel A. Poling

Yesterday San Francisco saw the faith of youth marching, in her avenues. One of your distinguished citizens stood there and as the young people went by he turned to a friend and said, "I did not believe it! I was sure there were comparatively few such young people. I did not believe it!"

He did not suppose that there was so much faith left in the world. That means something to us, does it not?

We are grateful for your presence in this convention. We understand what it means. We know that beyond any message that may be brought from this platform, your lives will be messages when you return. You can never be the same again. You have been changed, permanently changed. And because you have been changed it is possible for you of this convention to change your communities and to help to change your world.

What is a warless world—the warless world that is to be?

It is the world of Christ's will; it is the world of His will and plan. "I am come that they might have life, and might have it more abundantly." That was His brave word. There can be no *abundant living* with the threat of war stalking east and west, and north and south. Little children suffer because of that threat. Men and women are hungry for bread, and do not have the fulfillment of life, because of that threat. Fear establishes the foundations of new forts. The warless world is Christ's will and Christ's plan. We are of His purpose when we give ourselves to that broad project.

Christian Endeavor is increasingly a demonstration for a warless world. We have our difficulties: we have our national problems. Patriotism begins at home. I have very frank suspicions of the individual who talks about internationalism in such fashion as not to place the emphasis first upon his responsibility as a citizen of San Francisco, or Los Angeles, or Chicago, or New York. Distance lends enchantment to the view, but it may also suggest relief from immediate obligations. I have similar suspicions of that particular individual who talks about a universal womanhood that does not begin in loyalty to his own wife.

But patriotism, which begins at home, does not end there. Patriotism is not enough! The words of Edith Cavell were well spoken— "We are citizens of God's world." And we, as Christian Endeavorers, in these relationships, are members of a world-wide fellowship—four million members in 126 nations or dominions or states or island groups; all the races represented; all languages.

Again and again I have come into conventions in other countries where it has been impossible for me to understand a single word that was spoken, and I have understood only as I have been fortunate in my interpreter.

I can see a great audience reaching out into the dark recesses of a great cathedral. I can see that audience, and I can feel its spirit rising to meet my message. My interpreter is a distinguished professor from a great university, a direct descendant of that bishop who crowned the first of the Hapsburgs, a doctor in his own right—having earned it in the universities of Europe.

I realized suddenly that whatever I might say, the passion of this man would carry it to the hearts of the people. I found that I forgot the necessities of the hour, forgot that I was doing the speaking, and watched his face as he took my poor words and flung them out upon the people gathered there. Sixteen hundred young men were at my left or in front of me. Sixteen hundred young people were at the right and in front. They were the children of martyrdom. A monument behind the church carries the names of the professors and clergymen who were sent to the gallows long ago. There came upon me there the weight of my debt for my own Christian faith, for which I have paid so little. Their very faces carried the testimony of this giving which was a part of their spirit and traditions.

So when I think of a warless world I think of these Hungarian Christian Endeavorers and of the German Christian Endeavorers. Wherever we go, we sing the same songs. Wherever we go, we study the same great Book of Books. Wherever we go, we follow in the name of Him whom, not having seen, we love. Wherever we go, the suffering face of Christ calls in terms of suffering and sacrifice from our lives. We are one. We are one at last. Whatever our differences may be, we are one because our unity is in Jesus Christ.

The peace that is to be perfect peace must at last centre in His great declaration: "By this shall all men know that ye are my disciples, if you have love one to another." We bring, therefore, our commitment to the machinery of peace. We pledge our support to the projects of understanding and good will.

The blood that binds us in the cause is the blood of Him who is the Captain of the great salvation. He calls us, and we follow Him. And in His name we present every challenge of this great convention.

The World Gospel

A brief address on evangelism and on the spirit of the Christian Endeavor movement was broadcast by Dr. Poling in the Youth Radio Conference of Thursday,—the final one of the series. Something more than an hour before, the delegates had received President Hoover's message by radio from the distant Capitol City. In the intervening hour, there were messages on "Youth and an Old Gospel" by Rev. Louis II. Evans, and "Youth and a New World" by Dr. Fred B. Fisher.

"We have been on a mountain-top," said Dr. Poling, referring to the convention sessions as a whole. He told of standing on a peak in the Cascades, when some of the party said, "Yes, it is good to be here, but there is work to do below."

"We go from our mountain-tops, not with regret, but with inspiration and the determination to make our lives count for others," said the speaker. "We will have courage now that we did not possess before. Now we can reach out to India and other distant lands with our influence. All the States of the Union must feel the fervor of the youth of this convention."

More questions than ever were answered in this period, in which Charles F. Evans, field representative of the International Society, presided. But even then, there were numerous queries that could not be reached. Some of these will be dealt with in the next series of Youth Radio Conferences, broadcast from New York through a national hook-up.

Without attempting to give all the questions answered, the following typical inquiries, and Dr. Poling's replies, are now quoted.

Convention Queries

"What is the creed of the Christian Endeavor Society?"

Christian Endeavor societies are organized in all evangelical churches. The societies do not have a creed or a statement of such, because the statement of belief for a Christian Endeavor society is the statement of belief subscribed to by the church, by the denomination, by the communion, in which the Christian Endeavor society has been organized and to which its members belong.

The Christian Endeavor interdenominational and international movement is not a governing body. It gives no orders. It is a servant. It is a clearing-house for ideas, a platform of common agreement, the great centre for inspirational leadership. These conventions bring together young people from the four corners of the continent and the far places of the earth. They are black and they are white; they speak all languages and practically all the minor dialects. They represent *all* the churches. They each owe first allegiance to the communion, the denomination, or the brotherhood with which each is associated.

Our common agreement together is that, "trusting in the Lord Jesus Christ for strength," we shall strive to do His will, having this vital and vitalizing evangelical faith.

"What is the question that you find occupying the minds of young people more than any other? What question do they ask you more often than any other?"

The question young people ask more than any other is: "Tell me how to succeed. What books shall I read, and what courses shall

I take? What shall I do to make my life count for most?" In one way or another, every young person, after his or her fashion, asks that question.

I recall a boy in Baltimore, Maryland, who wrote to me saying that he wanted to be a great football player. "But," he said, "I am yellow. I am afraid to run with the ball. I am afraid to tackle. Is there anything that I can eat that you know of that might help me to develop courage? I am yellow, but I want to be a great football player."

I wrote back to that lad, and said: "You are not yellow; you are honest. I know what you are talking about, for I have passed through that experience myself. Courage, after all, is seldom an inheritance. It is generally acquired."

I told him to go out and run with the ball; I told him to tackle. I told him to adopt as his motto, "The man who can is the man who will." That some of the finest courage ever developed was that not of men who had proper food but of those who were starving to death—those who had little or no food—but who went through the wilderness and through the storm facing enemies and doing the work that had been assigned to them, and that made possible the large achievements of the pioneers.

Yes, that is the question. What must I do to learn how to run with the ball?

What must I do to succeed in business? in the home? in friendship? in government? in the church? That is the question we are all asking, I am sure; for each one of us is anxious to make his or her life count for the most. Christian Endeavor says, "Trusting in the Lord Jesus Christ for strength, I promise Him that I will strive to do whatever He would like to have me do."

"Are not young people today more inconsiderate of older people than formerly? You say you believe in youth, but I could tell you some things!"

Believe me, you could! Anybody can. Are young people more inconsiderate? Yes, some young people are, just as some young people used to be. In general, I find young people at this point reflecting the attitude of the older people with whom they associate. The most considerate people I know on earth are young people.

"There are two boys who ruin our society. One is foolish, and the other rides his ultra notions. How can we manage them?"

These boys might better be in the society than outside. If you can not solve this problem at short range, knowing the individuals, you are not fit to be a leader. Give these boys things to do. Deal frankly with them.

"I am a young man of twenty. My parents cannot afford to send me to college. I have been accepted by a certain college, but they have not been able to find employment for me. Therefore, it seems impossible for me to go, but still the urge and desire to go is so strong that I feel there must be some way of going. What do you advise?"

Some of our most important educators believe that fifty per cent of those in college today should be elsewhere. Certainly too many look upon four years in college as an extended vacation, with an opportunity for the sort of living that does not build into a program of constructive activity afterward. When I receive a question like this, then, I know that there remains that vast number of young people who with eagerness would prepare themselves for life. I am glad to tell you that after the freshman year there are funds available in student loans, from a number of the foundations, and from an increasingly larger number of colleges. If the one who has asked this question will give me not only the name, but the address, I shall be able to be of some service in that direction.

Beyond this it seems possible, as in my day, for young men to work their way through, particularly if the institution to which the young man would like to go may not be in a position at this moment to render assistance. But here again, if I may have the name and address, I may be of some assistance. If this young man has not only the determination indicated by the question, but good health and a reasonable amount of ability, and has not got beyond the college age altogether, I can almost guarantee him success in his heart's desire.

"What should be one's attitude toward nicknames?"

A boy is unfortunate if he does not have a nickname. Often the nickname means more than the real name.

"Why do we say, 'Blessed are the meek'? Don't the meek usually get stepped on?"

Jesus knew what He was talking about. Sometimes we do not understand how His words should be received. In Xenophon "meek horses" are spoken of. They were trained horses, spirited but controlled. In this sense the disciplined, the self-controlled, shall surely and inevitably "inherit the earth."

From an Intermediate Christian Endeavorer: *"Do you think it wise for an Intermediate to make a public decision for full-time service, as some seem to forget their decisions except in public?"*

I think the matter of full-time decision is vital. We should not present the appeal of full-time service, the program of the Life-Work Recruit, so as to secure a mass response or to encourage that. I prefer the plan that brings the young person into consultation with the pastor, that makes possible interviews with responsible leaders, that indicates the burdens that must be borne and the hard trials that must be experienced and the long years of preparation that must be passed through.

At the same time, let me say nothing that will indicate that I do not understand that again and again boys and girls hear the voice, and catch the gleam, and come to know the will of God. My decision with regard to this very matter was made long before I completed my college course.

We do need wisdom in our leadership today, and I am happy to believe that more and more in our churches, as well as within our denominations, we are giving a comprehensive, adequate leadership to the boys and girls of the Intermediate ages with regard to full-time service.

"If prohibition is so good a thing, why is there so much discussion? Will it work?"

I say to you, as was said by Dr. Mark A. Matthews from this platform, that prohibition at its worst is immeasurably better than was the old license system at its best.

Why is it necessary to discuss it? Because there are always some who would break the law because it is to their advantage that it be broken; because from the financial standpoint, or from the standpoint of appetite to be satisfied, they prefer to break it. They would rather break the law than keep it.

We have two kinds of law: mandatory law and permissive law.

Permissive law tells a man what he may do, what he wants to do. Mandatory law tells us some things that must not be done. Also there are some people, face to face with a mandatory law, who want to do the particular things prohibited. Mandatory laws must be enforced. Mandatory law is not an automatic machine; it is a tool, a good tool; but it must be used.

You can stand an axe by the side of a California redwood and allow it to stand there for a generation without effect upon the tree. But put your hands about the axe, and swing it against the tree in proper fashion, and eventually the tree comes down. Prohibition is mandatory law. It represents opportunity. We believe it to be the expressed will of a great majority of the American people. And in proportion as that law is used, in proportion as that law is accepted as opportunity, in proportion as that law is enforced and observed, it will affect increasingly the life of the citizens of the United States, and presently, through its influence, the life of the world.

WILLIAM SHAW, LL. D.
*Former General Secretary of
the International Society*

CHAPTER IX

GOLDEN MEMORY MOMENTS

Dr. Grose's Tributes to Dr. Clark and Dr. Poling—"Dreams
and Visions" Comes from the Gifted Pen of Dr.
William Shaw—Mrs. Clark Is Honored by
Seven Hundred Young Members
and Alumni

TWO messages from the rich experiences and memories of
veteran Christian Endeavor leaders are those addressed to
Dr. Poling and the convention by Dr. Howard B. Grose and
Dr. William Shaw. The record of the Golden Jubilee Convention would be incomplete without the presentation of these
stirring papers by two statesmen of the movement who were
invited to speak in person but for reasons of health could not
attend the San Francisco meetings.

Dr. Howard B. Grose, editor of "Missions," magazine of
the Northern Baptist churches, was ordained to the ministry in
1883. He was one of the first pastors to find and use the new
Christian Endeavor idea for young people's work in his own
church. He has been minister, college professor, university
president, and editor, and for many years has been vice-president of the International Society of Christian Endeavor. Dr.
Grose is perhaps best known to us as designer of the familiar
Christian Endeavor monogram and as co-author of Christian
Endeavor's most famous citizenship slogan—the 1911 Convention objective, "A Saloonless Nation by 1920."

A GOLDEN ANNIVERSARY MESSAGE

By Dr. Howard B. Grose

One date is indelibly fixed in the religious history of American
youth—February 2, 1881. That was the birthday of the Young
People's Society of Christian Endeavor, the most significant, far-
reaching, and influential youth movement of spiritual character and
purpose in Protestant church history.

Fifty eventful years of Christian Endeavor! I suppose that those
of us whose memories go back to the days of beginnings find a peculiar
satisfaction in reminiscence. Memory has for me no greater delight

than to enable me to relive those July days of 1885 at Old Orchard, when in the little chapel in the Maine pines the United Society of Christian Endeavor was born. Vivid is the picture of that eager, earnest company, listening closely to the young pastor of Williston Church as he unfolded the idea and genesis of the young people's movement of which he was the founder.

Of one thing I am sure, as I think back, that neither he nor any of us who were associated with him that day had the remotest conception of the illimitable power within the movement we were setting in motion—a movement, in truth, which after fifty years has not yet been fully comprehended. But we felt we were in a good work. There was something indefinable but inspiring in the atmosphere of that first meeting. There was an informality, a friendliness, an alert interest, a brotherly spirit such as I had not known before. And I have found that spirit animating Christian Endeavor meetings and associations during all the years since.

I discovered the secret of it later when I came to realize that the inspiring source of it was the radiant personality of Francis E. Clark, who was a veritable spring of vitality. He bred the fellowship of a common purpose, a *cameraderie* of service. I wish to emphasize strongly the fact that in reverence, in modesty, in altruistic idealism, and in definite spiritual aims for the development of character, Christian Endeavor started right, and through all the years has held unswervingly to its ideal.

Many of us caught the vision of a natural and happy Christian life and of a new world of church activities for young people that day, and I would that I might impart to the Endeavorers of today something of the thrill and quickened heartbeat that made that first convention forever memorable. That the same zest and joy in service abide still in Christian Endeavor prove its imperishable vitality. One thing I know—I went back to my church and young people a confirmed devotee of Christian Endeavor, and I haven't got over it yet after these nearly fifty years—nor ever shall. At Old Orchard I had made a life-long friend.

The Impress of Personality

What a unique leadership was his! One of the phenomenal facts of the phenomenal Christian Endeavor movement was the way in which from the first days to the close of his life Francis E. Clark permeated it with his personality. The name that soon came to be familiar everywhere—Father Endeavor Clark—was not a mere nickname but the expression of a relation that linked the founder and the Society indissolubly in the thought of the millions enrolled under the Christian Endeavor banner in all lands.

His leadership was natural and inevitable. He did not seek it nor could he escape it. As the Movement grew he grew with it. And as he traveled around the world again and again the extent of his personal acquaintance and influence increased until undoubtedly it had no equal in human annals. Spared to give active leadership for more than forty years, through all vicissitudes, he held Christian Endeavor true to its motto, "For Christ and the Church," and by his own absolute loyalty to his Master, Saviour and Lord, left an ineffaceable stamp upon the movement to which his life was given. He had the joy also of choosing his successor and co-operating with him in new advances.

What a benediction you have in the presence of Mother Endeavor Clark, beloved by us all, his life partner and stay! We look back upon an amazing record. Only one point can I note here. Christian Endeavor introduced an astonished world to the era of big conventions, which aroused the interest not only of Christian young people and the church but of the public generally as well, as nothing else had ever done.

Millions of our young people owe to these conventions their opportunity to visit the leading cities and become acquainted with their country. It was the Christian Endeavor Convention in San Francisco in 1897 that first took me across the continent and revealed to me the vastness and glorious beauties of my native land and the larger meanings of American citizenship. Those convention trains bearing the Endeavor banners and forming a living line of light from coast to coast caught the popular imagination as no religious pilgrimage had ever done before. Who that was there could ever forget the unexampled welcomes and receptions which were given the Endeavorers along the way, the climax coming when at every appointed stop the cars were filled with flowers and fruit in profusion, and such fruit as most of the travelers had never seen or eaten!

The Christian Endeavor young people, with their happy faces, bright ways and cheery atmosphere, found immediate favor with the people everywhere. I am sure San Francisco will find the same radiant atmosphere and infectious cheer in the convention this anniversary year, and will have reason to rejoice that Christian Endeavor has once more accepted its warm-hearted hospitality.

Looking Forward with Youth

But while it is pleasant to recall such a past as Christian Endeavor presents, I do not live in the past. The present is too inviting and pressing. And while it is profitable for a great world movement like ours to take time for review, yet Christian Endeavor has ever been forward looking and forward marching.

As a wise leader, Dr. Clark in his convention messages laid before the Society a program for the future, and in this custom President Poling has followed him, with that keen insight into the signs and needs of the times and that rare ability for leadership that Dr. Clark saw in him first, and the rest of us afterward.

When I first heard about Dan Poling (he was Dan then, for they hadn't yet doctored and degreed him), it was as a live-wire temperance orator in Ohio, where he was giving the saloonkeepers plenty to worry about. He had also had a thorough training in Christian Endeavor, and Dr. Clark, who was always on the lookout for men, got his eye on him, just as he had aforetime fixed it on John Willis Baer of beloved memory, and on William Shaw, witty radiator of good cheer.

When in the course of time and events the mantle of Dr. Clark's unique leadership of the young people of the world fell upon Dr. Poling, he found that the most critical and vital issue—moral, economic, social and religious—confronting the nation was prohibition, the reform for which he had so valiantly and successfully fought in Ohio years before.

Was this not more than a mere coincidence? Was he wrong in the conviction that Christian Endeavor had come to the kingdom for such a time as this? Was he wrong in thinking that among the moral and spiritual forces to be enlisted on the side of righteousness and the home in this impending and titanic contest the millions of young people in the ranks of Christian Endeavor would form one of the most impressive, important and effective divisions? I do not think he was. I see a distinct providence in this coming together of the hour, the man, and the human power for a signal triumph of Christian citizenship in our country.

My dominant purpose in sending you this message is that I may make it clear to you all that I am with Dr. Poling, heart and soul, in this splendid call of his upon you for a new adventure in Christian citizenship—a call which has already aroused comment and concern among the foes of prohibition, and awakened a profound interest in the Christian people of our own and other lands.

As I see it, from the veteran's angle, Christian Endeavor has for fifty years been preparing the way among the young people of the Protestant churches for such a momentous movement as this. It has created the spirit of interdenominational unity, friendship and sympathy, and effected the personal acquaintance and the practical working together which have made it possible to enlist in voluntary and individualistic yet single and inexorable aim and purpose a mighty company of the best young people of the nation, intent on waging a winning campaign for righteous government and respect for and obedience to the law. Not by the concerted action of organizations as such—church or society—but by the independent action of trained and intelligent members who own Jesus Christ as Master and Lord and follow in His train, shall the enlightened and inspired hosts of an irresistible Christian citizenship move steadily forward to victory.

Holding this belief, I see Christian Endeavor in the front rank, in response to the call and duty of the hour. And believing with me, as I am sure you do, that every Christian Endeavorer has a part to play in this vital contest, I feel that you join me also in the conviction that in Christian Endeavor's president of today we have one worthy to lead not only the forces of Endeavor but the people of America in such a time as this. Wherefore, with one voice let us say, all hail to President Poling and the coming campaign for humanity and the right!

Looking Both Ways

That Christian Endeavor's past is but an earnest of its future growth and possibilities was also the central theme of the splendid message of Dr. William Shaw, which follows. Dr. Shaw was Christian Endeavor's long-time International General Secretary,—"the great field marshal of our golden past," as Dr. Poling has said. Retired and living happily in a garden spot on the west coast, Dr. Shaw has been in good health until a few weeks before the San Francisco Convention, and it was a source of great regret to this veteran administrator of the young people's movement and to his host of friends that he could not attend the Golden Jubilee sessions.

William Shaw ("Billy the Blessed" they have called him), left a blossoming business career to enter the life work of Christian leadership in 1886, after serving Christian Endeavor since 1883 in a part-time capacity. He was for many years publisher of THE CHRISTIAN ENDEAVOR WORLD and was General Secretary for fifteen years.

DREAMS AND VISIONS

From the Message of Dr. William Shaw

I go back in my dreams forty-eight years, and see that little group of fifty societies, with 2,500 members, all there was of Christian Endeavor when I joined its ranks. I see the sowing of the seed on six continents and in the far-flung islands of the seas. I count the societies by scores of thousands and the members by millions, of every tribe and tongue and color and condition, the wide world around.

They are young people filled with the fervor of youth, for whom the church once made no place in her program. But they dared to claim their rightful place in spite of criticism and opposition from their elders.

Christian Endeavor was born in an era of intense denomination-alism. Yet it coined the new word, "interdenominational," and boldly inscribed upon its banners, "One is your Master, even Christ, and all ye are brethren."

All Races in This Brotherhood

Christian Endeavor is convinced that no picture of the kingdom of God is adequate if it consists of nothing but a white background. It insists upon the inclusion of the blacks and yellows and reds and browns, and all the shades in between. It has stood from the beginning, without apology and without compromise, for inter-racial fellowship and international brotherhood.

But principles without personalities are cold and lifeless. It has been said that "every great movement is but the lengthened shadow of a man." This is doubly true of Christian Endeavor, which is the lengthened shadow of a man and a woman, Dr. Francis E. Clark, and his devoted wife, Harriet Abbott Clark. I knew Mrs. Clark first, for she was my teacher for six months in the grammar school in Ballard Vale, Mass. She was a frail young girl; and how we young wildcats tormented and tried her, in ways that would have discouraged one of less indomitable spirit!

But this girl became the woman who was to be the comfort and support and inspiration of Dr. Clark for more than fifty years. Without a murmur she sent him away on his world-wide journeys in the interests of Christian Endeavor, while she remained at home to care for the children; or she accompanied him and shared the perils and hardships by sea and land.

To many of you Dr. Clark is but a name. But to me he was first my pastor (and an ideal one, who believed in his young people and appealed to the heroic in them) and then my chief and leader in the wider field of Christian Endeavor; and what a privilege it was to serve under such a leader! How strong and gracious and winsome a personality was his! So wise in all his plans, so eager to pass on to others the credit for things accomplished, so ready to take the heavy end of every task, and always leading in service and self-sacrifice.

A Pioneer in Great Tasks

Christian Endeavor sponsored the first studies in Christian citizenship (and coined that term), prepared by that veteran leader in civic and social service, Professor Graham Taylor, who has just celebrated his eightieth birthday.

In Troy, N. Y., there stands a monument to the memory of Robert Ross, the Endeavorer who died a martyr to his Christian-citizenship principles.

Christian Endeavor issued the first of the series of Systematic Bible-Studies, prepared by Professor William R. Harper of Yale University, later president of the University of Chicago.

It organized the first mission-study clubs, under the leadership of our own Professor Amos R. Wells and S. L. Mershon, which later, with the co-operation of Earl Taylor of the Epworth League, led to the organization of the Young People's Missionary Movement.

And Christian Endeavor united the moral-reform forces of the nation with the inspiring slogan, adopted at the Atlantic City Convention in 1911, "A Saloonless Nation by 1920." There followed the almost unanimous adoption of the Eighteenth Amendment by the States.

Government by the Criminal?

Some of us have been in the business of educating the public on the evils of the drink traffic for more than fifty years. That is just what the Prohibition party, the Woman's Christian Temperance Union, the Anti-Saloon League, the Catholic Temperance Society, the Sons of Temperance, the Good Templars, Father Mathew, Francis Murphy, John B. Gough, Frances E. Willard, the religious and temperance press, the public schools, and our churches, Sunday schools, and young people's societies have been doing the past century. There has been no help by voice or pen from these prominent wets of high society who now pose before the public as the real friends of temperance, and class us as hypocrites and fanatics.

The results of our educational campaign were the Eighteenth Amendment and the Volstead law, which they have opposed, misrepresented, or defied from the beginning. The simple fact is that they do not believe in, or want, the prohibition of the liquor traffic, and we do—and intend to have it.

May I remind you that the greatest question before the American people today is not the problem of prohibition, but whether this nation, fathered by Washington and defended by Lincoln with his life's blood, is to continue to be "a government of the people, by the people, and for the people," or is to become a government of the criminal, by the criminal, and for the criminal?

Our government today is opposed by an armed conspiracy of aliens and traitors within her borders.

All hail to the Allied Forces, the new movement that is uniting the people of the nation, including its young people, for the defence of their national heritage of "liberty under the law."

New Goals for Daily Work

The world of tomorrow is to be your world, and you have a right to a voice in the decision as to the kind of world it shall be. Industry and commerce have tried the competitive system, and it has failed. Register your demand for a test of co-operation. Making money has been the goal. It is for you to insist that making men shall be the first consideration.

Nations have tried war as a solution for their problems, and have poured out their treasure in billions of dollars, and sacrificed millions of lives to pay the bills. In spite of the tragic lessons of the World War the nations are today spending more money and training more men in preparation for another war than ever before in the history of the world.

In the name of a loving Father and of His suffering children you who supply the cannon-fodder must insist that this insane foolishness stop. Register your demand that the nations shall now try peace as their policy, with arbitration and a world court as instruments.

The church has tried to win the world under the banners of denominationalism, and has failed. Register your demand that we get together under the banner of Christ, and by our unity proclaim Him as the world's only and sufficient Saviour.

Hear the challenging words of the Master as He closed His earthly ministry:

"That they all may be one; as thou, Father, art in me, and I in thee, that they also may be one in us; that the world may believe that thou hast sent me."

The Birth of Christian Endeavor

An article that Dr. Francis E. Clark wrote in Australia in 1892, describing the early days of Christian Endeavor, and comparing the society to a growing infant and child, was read by Mrs. Clark in one of the most joyous of the fellowship meetings of the Golden Jubilee Convention.

This was a banquet of Alumni and younger Christian Endeavorers, seven hundred in all, held Wednesday evening, July 15, at the Whitcomb Hotel. Mrs. Clark was the guest of honor.

Those who spoke briefly in tribute to Mrs. Clark in advance of her own unforgettable remarks, include Chairman Carlton M. Sherwood, Dr. Daniel A. Poling, Dr. William Hiram Foulkes, Colonel Raymond Robins, Fred D. Parr, Harry N. Holmes, Bishop Fred B. Fisher, and Rev. Wallace J. Anderson, who is president of the Korean Christian Endeavor Union. Flowers were presented by the mid-west secretaries and fruit by the Oregon Christian Endeavor Union.

Mrs. Clark did not let the occasion become emotional. With the tact and wisdom so characteristic of her she began her own remarks to the delegates and older friends by poking fun at those who considered her old and weak. "My elbow has been carried for me all the way across this continent," she said, and told three stories about the alleged weakness of elderly people that literally convulsed her audience.

Then, in sober vein, Mrs. Clark thanked Mrs. Poling and the many others who had done multitudes of pleasant things for her in her journey to the Golden Jubilee Convention.

Dr. Clark's article, from which she read, follows:

"There is not much to tell of that little babe which was born in 1881. It was born on a very cold night in February at the pastor's residence, and like most other babes, attracted no notice and very little interest outside its own home.

"It was scarcely born when it began to use its voice, and in this it resembled most other babes. Like them, too, its articulation was just what was suitable to its years. No speeches nor efforts of rhetoric, because that would be unnatural, and would kill any society, old or young, but very simple and very brief words of confession for the Master.

"Soon it began to use its eyes. It began to see many open doors for service, it began to notice what might be amended, many opportunities for saying a kind word or doing a kind deed.

"With perception came also the desire to act, and it began to use its hands in many ways, and its feet in going upon many errands of loving service.

"Then bye and bye its brain began to be used. Better and more acceptable ways of doing God's work began to be considered and adopted. Consecrated intelligence was necessary in the highest paths of Christian service. Our reason and intelligence should be used and developed in this service.

"And so the young child learned to use its voice, its hands, its feet and brain, simply at first, as became its years, yet with ever increasing confidence and success.

"But it never forgot that it had a heart, and that its heart was its most precious possession. Its heart was the monthly consecration meeting. There, in all humbleness and sincerity it approached the common God and Father of us all, and with simple words of consecration re-dedicated every faculty and every opportunity to the Master."

RECOLLECTIONS OF FRANCIS E. CLARK

Told by John F. Cowan, his associate for twenty years and more.

In the early Eighties I first met him at a convention at Grafton, West Virginia, where I had the honor to speak on the same program. I remember my first impression, as I met him at the train—a tall, slender, youthful-appearing man, with dark hair and long "Burnsides." He had a most genial smile and friendly eyes and voice. I liked him from the first moment.

You might enjoy one figure of speech in his address. Referring to criticisms of Christian Endeavor, then but a few years old, that it meant over-organization of the church, he said that the oyster is the simplest organism, while man, the crown of creation, is the most complex. He could not think that the Head of the church would want it organized like the oyster, rather than like man.

That night we were entertained together in a private home (J. W. Hull's), and slept in the same bed. He talked about my forthcoming book, "Endeavor Doin's Down to the Corners," and advised D. Lothrop Co., as publishers.

Later, in a gathering of world Congregationalists, in Tremont Temple, Boston, a British minister criticized severely the Junior Christian Endeavor Society. Dr. Clark was the gentlest and most courteous of men, but when Christian Endeavor was hostilely and unfairly attacked he could spring to its defense like a mother whose child was threatened by a savage dog. He arose on the floor and asked permission to reply. As he could not be seen there, calls came: "Take the platform!" But he was too intensely concerned to waste a moment, so stood on two chairs and answered the attack with vigor and warmth that won a round of applause.

But usually he was the soul of graciousness and courtesy. For a number of years my office in the Christian Endeavor headquarters adjoined his. Through the connecting door, often ajar, I could easily hear him dictating to his secretary, or conversing with visitors. Always his voice was kindly in its inflections. He was tenderly considerate of others. At lunch together, travelling on trains, steamships, in the hurry and strain of affairs, he was ever the kind of a man who can be a "hero to his valet." Yet he was of statesmanlike calibre, meeting in his travels nobility and royalty with the grace of a courtier and never snobbish to the least.

Sometimes the little office prayer-meeting would be led by our colored janitor, and next week by Dr. Clark, always with an appreciative word for the preceding leader. He saw nothing incongruous in it; he was the most democratic and humble of men. The last time I was his guest, at his beach cottage, we walked together to his garden, dug potatoes and picked beans and cucumbers for the dinner.

Another incident shows his intense, self-sacrificing devotion to the service he was giving to youth. While still convalescing from typhoid, and weak, he had started for China to fill important Christian Endeavor engagements. As he and Mrs. Clark tarried at Honolulu, I journeyed there from my home on another island to see them. His pale, emaciated form and the weakness of body and voice made me fear for such a strenuous program. I begged him to go home with me and rest a month, for that long, hard trip. His answer was: "But they are expecting me. I must go on trusting God."

I bade them good-bye feeling I should never see him again on earth. He did have a relapse and pneumonia, but was spared for a number of years of that same unsparing loyalty to the cause he so loved.

The last time I saw him was as we played shuffle-board together on the deck of the steamship returning from the London Convention. He scarce had strength to shove the disks to the goal, but all through the voyage he never missed meeting with the Christian Endeavorers in their ship devotions, mingling with them on deck, and always with that lifelong, genuine, kindly interest.

What a prince of man he was! Travelling the circumference of the earth a dozen times to further religion among young people of the globe; writing two-score of books; editing a great religious paper; meeting with prime ministers; speaking in colleges and universities, honored, feted, sought after, yet when he spent a Sunday with John Wanamaker, Cabinet member, in his Philadelphia home and Sunday-school, he climbed tenement-house stairs until his muscles ached, to visit a sick scholar or an immigrant girl.

In all the forty and more years it was my privilege to know him he seemed to me more like his Master in spirit than any other man I have ever been privileged to know, and memories of him have a sweet, fragrant benediction.

HOWARD L. BROWN
*Field Secretary for the California
Christian Endeavor Union,
which entertained the
Convention*

CHAPTER X

RICH VALUES IN THE CONFERENCES

A New and Broader Educational Plan Is Introduced—One Hundred Hours of the Convention Time Is Invested in Discussing Religious and Social Issues and in Sharing Ideas and Methods for Christian Work

RICH and practical in conference material was the convention. Two types of educational needs were recognized in the more than forty conference sessions held each morning from Monday, July 13, to Thursday. July 16, the last four days of the six days' convention.

The religious and civic and social questions of the day, the genuine problems of church and state today, were outlined and discussed by youth under competent leadership in sixteen simultaneous sessions, held for one hour each morning, immediately following the quiet-hour service.

There followed the second one-hour period, in which approximately twenty-five groups met daily to outline and discuss both principles and methods of many forms of young people's religious activities.

For Sharing Points of View

The forums of the convention were closely allied to the main emphases of the evening sessions, in which leaders of international thought and action brought messages to thousands of young people. In the four hours of forum time available to each age group the points of view of young people from all parts of North America were expressed and discussed. Some of the principal speakers of the convention were themselves leaders of these daily forums, with groups of two hundred to three hundred or more attending some of these sessions.

In the forums the themes were "Sharing Christ with Others," "Christian Citizenship and a Christian Social Order," "International Good Will and World-Peace," and "The Gospel with a United Church Around the World."

The division of the convention delegates into forum groups was primarily by age. There were provided three conferences for those of twelve to fourteen years of age, three for those of fifteen to seventeen, five for those of eighteen to twenty-four, and five for those more than twenty-four years of age.

The printed program did not assign forum-leaders in such a manner that the delegates could select his conference according to the personality or popularity of the particular leader. Instead, only faculty members knew which one of the group of leaders listed would be in conference number five, for instance. This departure, one of the many in this year's conference arrangements, seemed so successful that it will doubtless be used in future International Conventions and in State conference programs as well.

School of Practical Methods

A service rendered particularly by Christian Endeavor conventions, district, State, and International, to young people, to societies and unions and to churches is the maintaining of practical educational sessions dealing with the why and the how of varied features of church-work.

A total of one hundred hours of such instruction, discussion, and exchange of ideas and experiences was provided in the school of methods of the San Francisco Convention. International Society officers, denominational leaders, field-secretaries of State unions, and volunteer officers, to the total number of thirty-two, shared in this leadership. Each conference had as chairman some young man or young woman, in most cases a field-officer or State union leader, who had a distinct contribution to make to the topic discussed.

Typical subjects for the second-period methods conferences follow:

Preparing for and Leading Society Meetings.
Informing the Public (Publicity).
Principles of Leadership.
Understanding and Practice of Worship.
Principles and Methods of Recreation.
Service Activities for the Society.
Missionary Education for Young People.
The Needs and Requirements of Christian Vocations.
Leading the Intermediate Age.
Principles and Methods of Union Work.
Leading the Junior Age.
Teaching Study-Classes in "Leadership through Christian Endeavor."
Principles and Methods of Religious Music and Song Direction.
Conference for Pastors and Directors of Religious Education.
Financing the Society and Personal Stewardship.
Christian Endeavor in a Total Church Program for Youth.

Leaders Met in Advance

The San Francisco newspaper men and women, an alert crew, found considerable news interest in the seven-o'clock breakfast of the International Christian Endeavor Convention's faculty, held daily during the final four days of the Golden Jubilee gathering.

Termed by the press "the president's breakfast," and considered as a parallel to the famous White House breakfasts of this and the preceding administration, this daily meeting of more than seventy leaders for mental and spiritual and physical refreshment was in fact a most significant occasion. Seated at tables in groups of four and eight, the chairman and conference-leaders and guest speakers of the convention had unusual opportunities to share their ideas regarding the work of the day and the significance of the previous day's session.

The group overflowed with valuable suggestions to make the convention features even more significant. Then each morning Rev. Harry Thomas Stock and Carlton M. Sherwood and others spoke, dealing with the theme of that day's forum sessions and with general suggestions for making the convention fruitful in both inspiration and information.

Dr. Poling, members of the local convention committee, and such leaders as Colonel Raymond Robins, Dr. Fred B. Fisher, Dr. C. Y. Cheng, and others, attended and participated in these early morning meetings. From the breakfast-room of the Hotel William Taylor the group went in a body to the auditorium to share in the daily quiet-hour services, led by Dr. William Hiram Foulkes. When the quiet-hour service adjourned at nine o'clock, the faculty and delegates gathered for two periods of discussion forums and methods conferences.

The Discussion Forums

Correlated with the main address themes of the convention were the forum themes of the four mornings. Each morning, in the first period, a major religious and social theme, of interest to young people, was presented in simultaneous sessions, in which the age groups were clearly recognized.

The arrangement and leadership of these simultaneous discussion groups will be seen in the following data, quoted from the "key list" that only faculty members received.

MONDAY	TUESDAY
"Sharing Christ with Others"	*"Christian Citizenship"*
(1) 12-14	(1) 12-14
Leader, Howard L. Brown	*Leader*, O. T. Anderson
Chairman, Louella Dyer	*Chairman*, Ethel Boxell
(2) 12-14	(2) 12-14
Leader, Charles F. Evans	*Leader*, Harold Singer
Chairman, Nettie Kilgore	*Chairman*, Lily King

(3)　12-14
　　Leader, Moses M. Shaw
　　Chairman, Elden Hobbs
(4)　15-17
　　Leader, Alvin J. Shartle
　　Chairman, Francis Mason
(5)　15-17
　　Leader, Paul C. Brown
　　Chairman, Glen Massman
(6)　15-17
　　Leader, Lawrence C. Little
　　Chairman, H. Lewis Mathewson
(7)　18-24
　　Leader, Harry Thomas Stock
　　Chairman, Willard E. Rice
(8)　18-24
　　Leader, J. Gordon Howard
　　Chairman, Hattie Mae Wood
(9)　18-24
　　Leader, Catherine Miller Balm
　　Chairman, James Henderson
(10)　18-24
　　Leader, Frank D. Getty
　　Chairman, Lily King
(11)　18-24
　　Leader, E. L. Reiner
　　Chairman, Ralph Rambo
(12)　Over 24
　　Leader, Jesse M. Bader
　　Chairman, Ernest S. Marks
(13)　Over 24
　　Leader, W. A. MacTaggart
　　Chairman, Russell J. Blair
(14)　Over 24
　　Leader, Homer Rodeheaver
　　Chairman, Roy Creighton
(15)　Over 24
　　Leader, E. W. Praetorius
　　Chairman, S. S. Morris
(16)　Over 24
　　Leader, Stanley B. Vandersall
　　Chairman, Aaron Brown

(3)　12-14
　　Leader, W. Roy Breg
　　Chairman, Aaron Brown
(4)　15-17
　　Leader, Walter W. Van Kirk
　　Chairman, Louella Dyer
(5)　15-17
　　Leader, E. L. Reiner
　　Chairman, Elden Hobbs
(6)　15-17
　　Leader, Bert H. Davis
　　Chairman, Elizabeth Cooper
(7)　18-24
　　Leader, Robert Ropp
　　Chairman, Russell J. Blair
(8)　18-24
　　Leader, J. Gordon Howard
　　Chairman, Warren G. Hoopes
(9)　18-24
　　Leader, Frank D. Getty
　　Chairman, Willard E. Rice
(10)　18-24
　　Leader, Harry N. Holmes
　　Chairman, Ross Guiley
(11)　18-24
　　Leader, Harry Thomas Stock
　　Chairman, Hattie Mae Wood
(12)　Over 24
　　Leader, Raymond Robins
　　Chairman, Herman A. Klahr
(13)　Over 24
　　Leader, T. T. Swearingen
　　Chairman, Alfred C. Crouch
(14)　Over 24
　　Leader, E. W. Praetorius
　　Chairman, S. S. Morris
(15)　Over 24
　　Leader, Ira Landrith
　　Chairman, Ralph Rambo
(16)　Over 24
　　Leader, Lawrence C. Little
　　Chairman, Glen Massman

WEDNESDAY

"International Good-will and World Peace"

(1)　12-14
　　Leader, Carroll M. Wright
　　Chairman, Francis Mason
(2)　12-14
　　Leader, W. Roy Breg
　　Chairman, Mrs. J. Q. Hook
(3)　12-14
　　Leader, Clifford Earle
　　Chairman, Lily King
(4)　15-17
　　Leader, T. T. Swearingen
　　Chairman, Russell J. Blair

THURSDAY

"A World Gospel and a United Church"

(1)　12-14
　　Leader, Paul C. Brown
　　Chairman, Marion Simms, Jr.
(2)　12-14
　　Leader, Willard E. Rice
　　Chairman, Elizabeth Cooper
(3)　12-14
　　Leader, Walter W. Van Kirk
　　Chairman, Lily King
(4)　15-17
　　Leader, Charles F. Evans
　　Chairman, Earl Israel

(5) 15-17
 Leader, O. T. Anderson
 Chairman, Glen Massman
(6) 15-17
 Leader, Harold Singer
 Chairman, S. S. Morris
(7) 18-24
 Leader, Harry Thomas Stock
 Chairman, Harold Lovitt
(8) 18-24
 Leader, Walter W. Van Kirk
 Chairman, Frederick L. Mintel
(9) 18-24
 Leader, Frank D. Getty
 Chairman, Warren G. Hoopes
(10) 18-24
 Leader, J. Gordon Howard
 Chairman, Ross Guiley
(11) 18-24
 Leader, Catherine Miller Balm
 Chairman, Howard L. Brown
(12) Over 24
 Leader, Harry N. Holmes
 Chairman, James Henderson
(13) Over 24
 Leader, Raymond Robins
 Chairman, Willard E. Rice
(14) Over 24
 Leader, W. A. MacTaggart
 Chairman, Ernest S. Marks
(15) Over 24
 Leader, Lawrence C. Little
 Chairman, Elden Hobbs
(16) Over 24
 Leader, Stanley B. Vandersall
 Chairman, Aaron Brown

(5) 15-17
 Leader, E. L. Reiner
 Chairman, Ernest S. Marks
(6) 15-17
 Leader, Moses M. Shaw
 Chairman, Warren G. Hoopes
(7) 18-24
 Leader, Harry Thomas Stock
 Chairman, Russell J. Blair
(8) 18-24
 Leader, Lawrence C. Little
 Chairman, Howard L. Brown
(9) 18-24
 Leader, Catherine Miller Balm
 Chairman, George Hamlin
(10) 18-24
 Leader, Frank D. Getty
 Chairman, Hattie Mae Wood
(11) 18-24
 Leader, J. Gordon Howard
 Chairman, James Henderson
(12) Over 24
 Leader, Stanley B. Vandersall
 Chairman, Glen Massman
(13) Over 24
 Leader. George H. Scofield
 Chairman, S. S. Morris
(14) Over 24
 Leader, E. W. Praetorius
 Chairman, Tephia Folsom
(15) Over 24
 Leader, W. A. MacTaggart
 Chairman, Clifford Earle
(16) Over 24
 Leader. A. J. Shartle
 Chairman. C. Fayette Lawrence

Principles and Methods

Practical help for young leaders and workers, and their pastors and counsellors, was provided in the large group of simultaneous methods conferences.

The emphasis in these second-period classes, as in the forums, was on sharing information and ideas. Leaders were chosen for their ability to guide discussion and exchange of ideas, rather than for a teacher's point-by-point presentation of the methods of church work. Weeks in advance, the leaders at the request of Carlton M. Sherwood submitted outlines of the general direction that the various conferences under their leadership would take. It was possible for the International Society staff officers, by studying these outlines, to have clearly in mind before the first conference opened what manner of instruction and discussion was likely to result. The delegates rose to their opportunities. Many of the conferees came away from the meetings wishing that they might go on for hours, so in'ense and vital had been the interest aroused.

These conventions have always abounded in the appeal to the

ideal and the definite training for the practical. As needs in youth work have broadened. conference programs have broadened to meet them. The Golden Jubilee Convention conferences are not the last word in methods instruction. They do represent an advance and incidentally their success had literally thousands of causes—the leadership and membership of the conference sessions!

The plan used for the second-period conference follows:

MONDAY and TUESDAY

(1) Preparing for and leading Society Meetings
High School Age
　　　Leader. Moses M. Shaw
　　　Chairman, Russell J. Blair
(2) Preparing for and leading Society Meetings
Over 18
　　　Leader, Harry Thomas Stock
　　　Chairman. Willard E. Rice
(3) Training Efficient Society Officers
High School Age
　　　Leader, C. C. Hamilton
　　　Chairman, Roy E. Creighton
(4) Training Efficient Society Officers ·
Over 18
　　　Leader, Frank D. Getty
　　　Chairman, George Hamlin
(5) Informing the Public (Publicity)
High School Age
　　　Leader, Ernest S. Marks
　　　Chairman, Nettie Kilgore
(6) Informing the Public (Publicity)
Over 18
　　　Leader, W. Roy Breg
　　　Chairman. C. Fayette Lawrence
(7) Principles of Leadership
High School Age
　　　Leader. Herman A. Klahr
　　　Chairman, Louella Dyer
(8) Principles of Leadership
Over 18
　　　Leader. J. Gordon Howard
　　　Chairman, Hattie Mae Wood
(9) Understanding and Practice of Worship
High School Age
　　　Leader, Clifford Earle
　　　Chairman, Ethel Boxell
(10) Understanding and Practice of Worship
Over 18
　　　Leader. T. T. Swearingen
　　　Chairman, Elizabeth Cooper
(11) Principles and Methods of Recreation
High School Age
　　　Leader, Catherine Miller Balm
　　　Chairman, Frederick L. Mintel
(12) Principles and Methods of Recreation
Over 18
　　　Leader, Carroll M. Wright
　　　Chairman, Marion Simms. Jr.

(13) Service Activities for the Society
High School Age
    Leader, Howard L. Brown
    Chairman, Alfred C. Crouch
(14) Service Activities for the Society
Over 18
    Leader, Charles F. Evans
    Chairman, Ralph Rambo
(15) Christian Endeavor in a total Church program for Youth
Over 18 only
    Leader, Lawrence C. Little
    Chairman, Willard E. Rice
(16) Leadership through Christian Endeavor
Over 18 only
    Leader, Bert H. Davis
    Chairman, S. S. Morris
(17) Missionary Education for Young People
High School Age
    Leader, O. T. Anderson
    Chairman, Aaron Brown
(18) Missionary Education for Young People
Over 18
    Leader, George Scofield
    Chairman, Francis Mason
(19) The Needs and Requirements of Christian Vocations
High School Age
    Leader, E. W. Praetorius
    Chairman, Russell J. Blair
(20) The Needs and Requirements of Christian Vocations
Over 18
    Leader, Stanley B. Vandersall
    Chairman, Tephia Folsom
(21) Leading the Intermediate Age
Intermediate Superintendents and counsellors
    Leader, Paul C. Brown
    Chairman, Lily King
(22) Leading the Junior Age
Junior Superintendents and interested adults
    Leader and Chairman, Mildreth J. Haggard
(23) Principles and Methods of Religious Music and Song Direction
Over 18
    Leader, Homer Rodeheaver
    Chairman, E. L. Reiner
(24) Principles and Methods of Christian Endeavor Union Work for
    all union officers
Monday   *Leaders*, Daniel A. Poling and Harold Singer
    Chairman, Carlton M. Sherwood
Tuesday   *Leader*, Harold M. Singer
    Chairman, A. J. Shartle

WEDNESDAY and THURSDAY

(1) Preparing for and Leading Society Meetings
High School Age
    Leader, Catherine Miller Balm
    Chairman, Howard L. Brown
(2) Preparing for and Leading Society Meetings
Over 18
    Leader, Clifford Earle
    Chairman, Lily King

(3) Recruiting and Training Members
High School Age
    Leader, Russell J. Blair
    Chairman, Elizabeth Cooper
(4) Recruiting and Training Members
Over 18
    Leader, A. J. Shartle
    Chairman, Alfred C. Crouch
(5) Financing the Society and Personal Stewardship
High School Age
    Leader, Warren G. Hoopes
    Chairman, Elden Hobbs
(6) Financing the Society and Personal Stewardship
Over 18
    Leader, Frederick L. Mintel
    Chairman, Louella Dyer
(7) Principles of Leadership
High School Age
    Leader, Willard E. Rice
    Chairman, Marion Simms, Jr.
(8) Principles of Leadership
Over 18
    Leader, Lawrence C. Little
    Chairman, Glen Massman
(9) Understanding and Practice of Worship
High School Age
    Leader, E. W. Praetorius
    Chairman, James Henderson
(10) Understanding and Practice of Worship
Over 18
    Leader, Harry Thomas Stock
    Chairman, Herman A. Klahr
(11) Principles and Methods of Recreation
High School Age
    Leader, Moses M. Shaw
    Chairman, Ernest S. Marks
(12) Principles and Methods of Recreation
Over 18
    Leader, Carroll M. Wright
    Chairman, Earl Israel
(13) Service Activities for the Society
High School Age
    Leader, J. Gordon Howard
    Chairman, Mary E. Jackson
(14) Service Activities for the Society
Over 18
    Leader, Harold Lovitt
    Chairman, Aaron Brown
(15) Christian Endeavor in a Total Church Program for Youth
Over 18 only
    Leader, Frank D. Getty
    Chairman, W. Arnett Gamble
(16) Leadership through Christian Endeavor
Over 18 only
    Leader, Bert H. Davis
    Chairman, S. S. Morris
(17) Missionary Education for Young People
High School Age
    Leader, Robert P. Anderson
    Chairman, Verna Harvey

(18) Missionary Education for Young People
Over 18
    Leader, Ross Guiley
    Chairman, George Hamlin
(19) The Needs and Requirements of Christian Vocations
High School Age
    Leader, O. T. Anderson
    Chairman, Louis B. Hillis
(20) The Needs and Requirements of Christian Vocations
Over 18
    Leader, Stanley B. Vandersall
    Chairman, Mrs. Howard L. Brown
(21) Leading the Intermediate Age
Intermediate Superintendents and counsellors only
    Leader, Paul C. Brown
    Chairman, Alfred C. Crouch
(22) Leading the Junior Age
Junior Superintendents and interested adults
    Leader and Chairman. Mildreth J. Haggard
(23) Principles and Methods of Religious Music and Song Direction
Over 18
    Leader, Homer Rodeheaver
    Chairman, E. L. Reiner
(24) Principles and Methods of Christian Endeavor Union Work
For all union officers
    Leader, W. Roy Breg
    Chairman, Charles F. Evans
(25) Principles and Methods of Christian Endeavor Union Work
For state officers only
Wednesday   *Leaders*. Daniel A. Poling and C. C. Hamilton
    Chairman. Carlton M. Sherwood
Thursday   *Leader*, Harold Singer
    Chairman. C. C. Hamilton

Typical Conference Material

(A few paragraphs from the many interesting reports of the
Golden Jubilee conferences.)

In a conference for leaders of Junior Christian Endeavorers, Rev.
E. L. Reiner, for nearly twenty years pastor of Waveland Avenue Congregational Church, Chicago, developed a number of interesting and
helpful points.

The leader told of a number of instances in which children of the
Junior ages came naturally to a Christian decision through the influence of a Christian home and the Sunday-school. It was brought out
in discussion that Billy Sunday figures, coming from a large meeting
in Chicago, showed that ten thousand of the twelve thousand present
had accepted Christ before the age of twenty. Nine thousand of these
had come to the church through the Sunday-school. Only one thousand of the number had accepted Christ between twenty and forty,
and but thirty-seven after forty. Revival meetings were commended.
provided the effort is followed up by personal work. "The personal
work and work of the Sunday-school teacher, Junior superintendent,
or minister avail much."

The pastor's class for young prospective members was also commended.

The first requirement for the song-leader is that he tear away
from his inferiority complex, suggested Homer Rodeheaver, in leading
a conference on religious song direction.

"Don't be afraid to take command of the situation," he counselled. "Dominate your group. Timid gestures fail, while emphatic gestures hold an audience, and make the leader's directions easier to follow."

The music should be subordinate to the message of the song used, he stated. It is important that pitch and tempo be such that undue effort is not required to carry out the mechanics of the selection used.

In its first session, Rev. O. T. Anderson's conference for young people of high-school ages dealt with the questions: Why do we have missions? What are the various kinds of missionary service? What are the methods of modern missionary enterprise?

The young people of the conference themselves determined these points:

1. Jesus commanded us to go.
2. Christianity has something worth sharing, something which other religions do not have.
3. Christianity is a religion of love, of courage, of strength. It has a needed message on the value of human personality.
4. The world needs Christ and His saving message.

Rev. J. Gordon Howard, of Dayton, Ohio, led a particularly interesting conference on the subject, "Around the World," dealing with all important phases of the missionary task.

One man used to do all the tasks. Now missionaries are specialists in one phase of the task, Mr. Howard explained. The new trend in missions is toward giving responsibility to the converts in the foreign field. The missionary guides and advises in the modern mission field. There are united churches now in Japan, China, India. Christian Endeavor is one of the chief agencies for unity both in foreign fields and among the American denominations.

Missionary work begins in us, the conference members agreed, and consists in sharing Christ with others. Whenever and wherever we share Christ, that is missions. The work will end only when every one knows Christ.

Included in the modern missionary task, the conference discovered, are:

1. Benevolent work.
2. Sanitation.
3. Education.
4. Medicine.
5. Agriculture.
6. Printing.
7. Literature.
8. Religious paper.
9. Government.
10. Preaching the gospel.

In one of a series of simultaneous conferences on missions, Rev. George H. Scofield, Ph. D., of Walla Walla, Washington, reminded the conference members that America is scarcely fifty per cent Christian in terms of population. "Read the lives of the modern apostles, the great preachers and missionaries of today," urged Dr. Scofield.

That the Christian ministery is now overcrowded was the conclusion voiced by Rev. Stanley B. Vandersall, Boston, Christian-Vocations superintendent of the International Society, in a conference on life-work choices. "On one hand we have vacant churches, which could not pay a living-wage," he said, "and on the other, unemployed ministers. Colleges are bringing out new recruits for the ministry more quickly than they can be absorbed."

An earnest group studied for four days' conference sessions, with Bert H. Davis, Utica, N. Y., as leader, the teaching of Mr. Davis's book, "Leadership through Christian Endeavor," to study classes. In one State union officers are recommending that each new member in a society receive a copy of this book so that he or she may learn the outlines of Christian Endeavor work without delay.

Provide wholesome recreation for the entire community! This goal for Christian Endeavor recreation committees in societies and unions was given by Carroll M. Wright, Boston, superintendent of the International Society's travel and recreation department.

"Especially in rural communities," said Mr. Wright, "it is often the function of Christian Endeavor groups to provide playgrounds and suitable reading material for young people."

The larger number of those present were familiar with the International Society's "Playtime" service, which appears regularly in THE CHRISTIAN ENDEAVOR WORLD. The same material is reissued by a number of State and local unions.

In another recreation conference session, Harry W. Githens, Quincy. Ill., a frequent contributor to THE WORLD, emphasized the importance of planning games in which everyone present may participate.

In one of the several conferences that dealt with service activities of the society, the following forms of service were proposed as the minimum for a successful season's program:

1. Lookout Committee getting new members and holding the old ones.

2. Missionary study class leading up to service projects, such as correspondence with missionaries, gifts to mission stations, and recruiting life-service members.

3. "Sunshine work"—visiting the sick, presenting fruit, flowers, and toys.

4. Joint sessions planned with other societies, including out of town societies.

5. Booster banquet, to keep up the fellowship and efficiency of a whole district or community.

6. Holding high school students' meetings, to recruit new members.

7. Emphasis on missionary giving, through denominational channels.

"The summer slump" was avoided in some societies by such plans as these—

1. Get back of some definite church objective.

2. Use varied programs and current-events topics, if desired.

3. Unite the meetings of several neighboring societies.

4. Welcome college students home on vacation and those visiting in the neighborhood to the meetings.

Training Efficient Society Officers

The goodly number of young people attending the conference for Society Officers, led by Clarence Hamilton, Publication Manager, showed that the leaders of our local societies were serious in their leadership and wanted to become efficient officers in their societies.

The conference brought out the fact that to be efficient leaders we must co-operate with the pastor, official board and Sunday School within the church, and with Denominations and Interdenominational Unions from without the church.

Mr. Hamilton introduced the Four Department Plan for a Christian Endeavor society suggesting that in these four departments— Prayer Meeting, Lookout, Missionary and Social—we cover every phase of Christian Endeavor work and give a job to every member of our society fitting the task to the individual.

The Pastors' Conferences

Not the least important of the score or more of daily conferences was that for pastors, led by Dr. Foulkes, on the platform of the main auditorium. Colonel Raymond Robins was the speaker on July 13. The main theme was world peace.

The speaker said: "We shall not really be living until we get rid of war. In measuring progress toward that goal we need to get the significance of the Kellogg-Briand Pact, to be known best as the World Peace Pact. It refers decisions as to wars to the sovereign people of nations, not to kings or dictators. Three months were spent on the phrase 'in the names of the respective people.' And weeks more were taken to secure the one word 'all'; it includes all disputes between nations."

Colonel Robins makes a sharp distinction between a "pacifist" and the word Jesus used, "peace-maker." He suggested that Henry Ford might try to get for his museum that log on the Rapidan River in Virginia on which President Hoover and Premier Ramsay Mac-Donald sat while pulling the two greatest nations on earth closer together, rather than some of the curios he has.

This Pact, he claimed, gives the peoples of the world "something to lean up against." The logical sequence of that Pact is the Permanent Court of International Justice at the Hague, the ratification of which by the United States is the next step ahead.

One of the big stakes involved is the six billion dollars spent yearly on armaments. We must see to it that when our delegates to the Geneva Armaments Conference are appointed, they shall not all be militarists; and he believes that President Hoover will listen to representations to that effect.

The second part of the session was spent in answers to questions, one of which was, "What is meant by the church's outlawing war?" The answer was that literally that is impossible; but President Hoover has spoken of creating a moral passion through religion, that sets fire to the conscience of the nation." We must roll up opinion show-ing that the people want disarmament.

Dr. William Hiram Foulkes, vice-president of the International Society of Christian Endeavor and pastor of the Old First Church, Newark, N. J., in a pastors' conference expressed his conviction that the young people of the present generation have been greatly maligned at the hands of unworthy critics. Instead of being corrupt and set upon evil, they are, on the whole, better than those of previous generations.

"There is a wide-spread tendency," said Dr. Foulkes, "to malign the rising generation. Unquestionably it is more frank than those that preceded it. It has not a few noisy members who take them-selves too seriously, and who are taken too seriously by their elders. On the whole, however, it is my observation, as one well conversant with the situation, that there is a rising tide of idealism in the heart of modern youth, which may not express itself in conventional forms.

"The so-called delinquencies of the present generation are largely those which have been handed to it by the passing generation. Middle-aged people are quite inclined to rail at young people simply because they perpetuate their own petty vices and moral faults.

"The Christian Endeavor movement after fifty years' intimate contact with an increasing number of young people announces itself as their whole-hearted champion, and earnestly seeks through its program the fullest co-operation of their lives in service for the whole world."

CHAPTER XI

QUIET HOURS AND DEVOTIONS

THE morning Quiet Hours, led by Rev. William Hiram Foulkes. D. D., LL. D., were most practical and helpful. Dr. Foulkes has established a nation-wide reputation as a leader of such meetings, and the four Quiet Hour services on the general theme, "Mountain Peaks with the Master," proved both uplifting and illuminating. The first talk, on Monday morning, was on

THE MODERN MOUNTAIN OF TEMPTATION

When youth is on the high mountain to-day, said Dr. Foulkes, its first temptation is to take short-cuts in the solution of economic problems. Temptation today, as in the days of Jesus, touches men on their strongest sides. The "get-rich-quick" craze destroys character.

The second temptation is to take a short-cut to success—to choose the spectacular way to win. Any career worth having, said the speaker, must be won. There are no easy ways to education, to real success, and to honorable business and professional standing.

The third form of temptation—power quickly obtained—had been particularly real to Jesus. He had a world-vision, that saw not merely Rome with its imperial greatness offered to him, but the other powerful nations that were and were to be. History is replete with stories of those that bartered their souls for power—Alexander, Caesar, Napoleon, impatient and ruthless masters.

Jesus divined that the world must be won by sacrifice. "Ye shall overcome the world because I have overcome" is the encouragement of the Christian who will not accept the short-cuts nor the spurious imitations of life.

THE MOUNT OF TRANSFIGURATION

Dr. Foulkes graphically defined the transfiguration as "Heaven breaking through, as if it could not contain itself." Jesus went to the mountain to pray. That must be presumed, for heaven could not reveal its glory to one whose face was not turned toward heaven.

The gospel gives only a fleeting flash of what took place that day; the imagination must supply the colorful, thrilling details. After all, the supreme glory of human life is revealed in the human face, not in a sunset, or a sunrise, or a Lake Tahoe or Louise.

There was a plain girl with a stolid face, unresponsive, expressionless. Then the light of love kindled in her heart broke out on that uninteresting face, and it began to shine with a radiance brighter than any ever seen on land or sea. That girl, so illuminated by the love of God, became a missionary in South America, and everywhere she went there are those who were touched and held and inspired by the love that shone on her transfigured face.

So Jesus went to the mountain top that His Father's glory might shine on His face. And that glory is undimmed to this day wherever

Jesus is honored and loved. We come to this convention to see the transfiguring glow on Jesus' face and to share in it. All depends on what lies behind our faces.

Look within! Is there sorrow for sin, longing, solicitude for grace and power to transform our lives? Yes, the object of this convention is to transfigure common lives. We are here to be transfigured with Jesus.

What are our associates and neighbors going to see in our faces hereafter? If they do not see in us all of the light that shone on that mount it will be because the current between Him and us is broken; but if they see a light of patience, of gentleness, of love not born of this world, then we shall be incandescent to them, as John described it, "burning and shining lights." And we can not shine unless we burn with ardor, self-sacrifice; we can not shine if the light is dimmed by sin within us. We can not go down into the valley and help others unless our eyes have been opened.

KINGLINESS CROSS-ENTHRONED

The offering of life for others may be finer and more exultant than any royal coronation.

Dr. Foulkes opened his talk on the crucifixion by quoting Renan: "The story of Jesus' suffering will always melt and uplift the human heart."

DELEGATES FROM GOLDEN RULE UNION, WASHINGTON, D. C.

He presented it in a fresh way, yet "true to the truth, sympathetically, tenderly, searchingly—the cross as a symbol of victory. It had a heroic appeal that conquered the thief, the Roman centurion, later Paul, and now one-third of the world's population. "The Old Rugged Cross" still has its powerful appeal; "rugged" Christianity will win.

The speaker pictured the death of Jesus as a seed-planting that "blossomed red" over all the world. We must not feel depressed and sad at thought of the cross. His cross was His glory, not humiliation or shame.

"I lay in dust life's glory dead,
And from the ground there blossoms red
Life that shall endless be."

The speaker reminded how lightly we treat the cross. We put it on our church spires and think we have done all. We dangle it on our watch chains, and wear it in brooches; but too often lose sight of its significance; we do not put it in our hearts. He illustrated by the story of Michael Blake who, spurned by his illegitimate son, went across seas to right the wrong. One on the ship said: "You do not wear a cross on your coat." And he replied: "No, I wear mine deeper."

Jesus' cross was deeper than His pierced hands and feet and riven side; it was pressed against His heart. Dr. Foulkes urged his hearers to allow conscience to cross-question them: "How near the cross am I? How much of its tragedy do I feel?" It is not enough to stand beneath its comforting, healing shadow. It bids us, "Come nearer; stretch out your hands; feel on your brow the crown of thorns; and the spear-thrust of the riven side."

We must be "crucified with Christ"; we must share His passion. What a pitiful thing it is to call a headache, or giving up something we like to eat, or wear, or do, a "cross!" What is the cross, literally? Jesus defined it as "denying himself;" it is saying "no" to self. It is easy to say "no" to others, but hard to say it to self; "no" to pride, fear, anger; hard to say "yes" to love and sacrifice. That is what crusading with Christ means. A crusader is a cross-bearer.

Dr. Foulkes closed by telling of an old monk who said: "The cross is large enough to crucify us all." It is large enough to rejoice all, to give all the glorious image of Him.

WITH JESUS ON FOUR MOUNTAINS

Dr. Foulkes, in his last Quiet Hour talk, introduced his theme by an incident from "Quo Vadis," in which Lew Wallace pictures the apostate Greek, seated, looking down on the martyrdom of Christians in the arena, and, being asked what he saw, answered in a tragic tone: "I see the resurrection."

In this series of talks, the mount of temptation, the mount of transfiguration, the mount of crucifixion had been seen; now the resurrection, and the Mount of Olives whence he ascended were in sight.

Notice was called to the fact that Jesus made special appearances for both Peter and Thomas—the man who was always pushing ahead and the man who was always lagging behind. To Peter He sent a separate message through Mary, and to Thomas after the Emmaus meeting He said, "Come hither and thrust in thy hand."

The speaker also compared the two confessions: Peter's "Thou art the Christ," and Thomas', "My Lord and my God!"

Another significant fact is that we see Jesus with Paul more than we do with Peter. Peter saw Him most on the other side of the resurrection, and Paul saw him on this side.

Dr. Foulkes, in a very impressive fashion, dramatized the resurrection scene—the adversary standing by on that morn, and Jesus demanding, "Let me through the gates of life." The adversary replying, "I cannot hinder thy deity, but leave behind thy humanity." But Jesus brought His humanity through, and is our brother.

The heart of the New Testament, it was stated, is in Paul's words: "I am crucified with Christ; nevertheless I live; yet not I, but Christ liveth in me." He asked: "Have you seen Christ here beside every speaker, beside Mother Clark? He has been here in ten thousand. And now, are we going to take Him and go where men and women, boys and girls, need him? If we go, obedient to His word, we have the assurance, 'Lo, I am with you always'."

CHAPTER XII

DENOMINATIONAL RALLIES

MONDAY afternoon was given exclusively to denominational meetings and rallies under accredited leaders of the different denominations. All the major denominations had large rallies, and the smaller denominations, although meeting in lesser groups, found that such meetings were well worth while.

The Presbyterian Church, U. S. A., had outlined one of the most ambitious and at the same time effective programs that we have ever seen at a denominational rally in a convention. The aim was not merely to talk to young people about Presbyterian work, but to show them missions in actual operation. We are indebted to Herman A. Klahr, of Cleveland, O., for the following excellent account of the day's doings among Presbyterians.

Presbyterian U. S. A., Rally

Almost five hundred Presbyterians participated in the Denominational rally. They assembled first at Presbyterian Headquarters

FRANK D. GETTY
*Philadelphia, Presbyterian
Board of Education*

MISS MILDRETH J. HAGGARD
Minneapolis, Junior Leader

(the Pacific Coast headquarters of Presbyterianism, including the Presbyterian book store) where buses were waiting to take them on a tour of Presbyterian mission centres. It was a joyous group. Virtually every State in the Union was represented.

The first stop was the Presbyterian Church of the Good Shepherd (Iglesia Presbyteriana el Buen Pastor). This is the only Protestant Spanish-speaking congregation in San Francisco. Although situated in the heart of a large foreign district, this church enjoys a wide ministry reaching into every section of the city and its environs. The visiting delegates had an opportunity to inspect the building, hear brief greetings from the pastor and young people's worker, and listen to special music provided by members of the church. Significant was the following testimony of the minister: "I know nothing except what the Presbyterian Church has taught me."

The next point of interest was the Potrero Hill Neighborhood House conducted for Russian children and young people. It is one of two neighborhood houses on the Pacific Coast. Well equipped and supervised by efficient personnel, this house conducts an outstanding work in the Russian quarter. The juvenile lockers, toilets, and shower bath were among many interesting items of equipment. As the delegates were ready for departure, following the tour of inspection, Russian girls served tea and wafers.

The last of the three centres to be visited was the Chinese Presbyterian Church. Here more than three hundred children and young people are served. Situated in the very heart of Chinatown, which is served by eleven denominations, this church occupies a unique position. The congregation is half self-supporting. Delegates met the

DR. W. A. MACTAGGART
Representing United
Church of Canada
Toronto

HOMER RODEHEAVER
Director of Song
New York

pastor, Rev. Tse Kei Yuen, and Miss Hubbard, the parish worker. The latter introduced us to groups of children who entertained us with gospel songs in both English and Chinese. The singing of "This is the end of a perfect day" was a fitting conclusion to the tour as we departed for Calvary Presbyterian Church, where dinner was served. Rev. Frank D. Getty, director of Presbyterian young people's work, presided. The singing was led by Paul C. Brown, Pacific Coast Secretary of Christian Endeavor. Time permitted only a few introductions, after which Dr. William Hiram Foulkes, Old First Church, Newark, N. J., Vice-President of the International Society, brought a brief but stirring challenge to the happy but serious banqueters.

Disciples of Christ Rally
By Rev. O. T. Anderson

The fellowship get-together of Disciples of Christ Endeavorers was held at the West Side Christian Church on Monday, July 13.

The general theme for the meeting was "Adventuring with Jesus." Four sub-topics of the theme were presented to the delegates, as follows:

1. "Adventures in Worship," by Wilbur Parry, religious education superintendent for Northern California.

2. "Adventuring through Study and Discussion," by T. T. Swearingen, national young peoples' superintendent. This was a presentation of the Disciples' young people's summer-conference movement.

3. "Adventures in Service," by Virgil A. Sly, associate secretary, department of religious education, United Christian Missionary Society.

Christian Endeavorers were asked to share in special missionary projects through the missionary organization of the communion.

4. "Adventuring With Jesus Around the World," by Dr. Royal J. Dye, a former medical missionary to Africa. There is no more dramatic speaker for the cause of missions today than Dr. Dye. In a challenging message, presenting the total missionary program of the church, he brought the afternoon to a climax.

About two hundred Endeavorers enjoyed the fellowship and inspiration of this rally.

Evangelical Congregational Rally

In our experience with denominational rallies we never found such an enthusiastic spirit among our people as was evidenced by our young folk. Greater things must be the outcome from these inspirational addresses and helpful thought-provoking conferences. There will be a return from this Jubilee Convention, a more loyal and devoted Christian Endeavor-loving people to witness and labor for the better things of life. Rev. P. D. Longsdorf, trustee, outlined how we can best serve our church.

From our representatives came the assurance that we will urge upon all our young people the high importance of qualifying in every possible preparation, so that we may occupy the place which the cause demands.

United Presbyterian Rally

One hundred sixty-nine United Presbyterians attended a luncheon in the Hotel William Taylor Monday noon, July 13.

William Orris Fisher, D. D., served as toastmaster, and addresses were made by President R. T. Campbell, D. D., of Sterling College, G. Ernest Raitt, D. D., synodical superintendent of missions for California, Rev. A. W. Webster, secretary of young people's work for San Francisco presbytery, and Moses M. Shaw, national secretary.

Attention was drawn to the annual meeting of the national council and the national convention in August when missionary and stewardship goals will be set and promotion plans outlined.

Delegates were given an auto trip through Golden Gate Park, the Presidio, and other points of interest.

The program provided for rallies of the following denominations, each with a well-known leader: First came the A. M. E. and A. M. E. Zion; then the Baptist rally, the Congregational and Christian Convention, the Church of God, Cumberland Presbyterian, Evangelical, Friends, Lutheran, Mennonite, Methodist Protestant, Moravian, Presbyterian U. S., Presbyterian Church of Canada, Primitive Methodist, Reformed Church in the U. S., Reformed Church in America, Reformed Presbyterian, Reformed Episcopal, Schwenkfelder, Seventh Day Baptist, United Brethren, United Brethren (Old Constitution), and the United Church of Canada. The rallies gave to denominational leaders an opportunity to present to the young people the program of their churches and to meet an inspired and informed group of leaders-to-be.

CHAPTER XII

WITH THE JUNIORS

THE Junior features of the San Francisco Convention were planned to allow a maximum of personal contact among the leaders and with the workers desiring information and counsel.

Junior headquarters were established in a lobby off the main corridor of the Auditorium and were indicated by a beautiful illuminated transparency in colors (showing the children of many nations), which had been made and mounted by Mrs. William V. Martin and Mr. Wilbert Martin of Illinois. With its comfortable furnishings, borrowed by the San Francisco Junior Committee, the profusion of fresh flowers, and the wealth of books, posters, and varied materials, new each day, this room proved most attractive as a service bureau. Here the local committee served as charming and faithful hostesses and were assisted by members of the Junior staff and the State Junior leaders.

For the tea on Sunday afternoon, at the dinner given on Monday evening by the International Society of Christian Endeavor for the State Junior superintendents, when Mrs. Francis E. Clark, Mrs. Daniel A. Poling, Mrs. Harold Singer, Mrs. Ella N. Wood, Mr. Carlton M. Sherwood, and Rev. Stanley B. Vandersall were our honored guests, and in the round-table conferences each morning, an inspiring group were present, consisting of the State leaders of all the Coast States—California, Oregon, Washington, and Arizona, and Utah, of representatives from Montana and Idaho, of State superintendents or their officially appointed representatives from North Carolina and Florida for the Southern States, from Illinois, Indiana, Minnesota, Kansas, Nebraska, Colorado, Missouri, and Texas of the Mid-West States, and from Massachusetts, New York, New Jersey, Pennsylvania, Ohio, West Virginia, and District of Columbia for the rest of the country.

These leaders studied the budgets of program and promotional materials from the various State Junior departments with a view to progressive program-building and more effective promotion. They consulted with the editor about the JUNIOR CHRISTIAN ENDEAVOR WORLD and with an expert in religious education about principles of Junior leadership. They discussed convention plans, the training of leaders, and available helps (many of which were really available for inspection) and then wished for as many more hours together.

The San Francisco Public Library afforded an unusually fine and convenient centre for the Junior conference activities of both hours and Mr. Ray, Librarian, and his staff co-operated in every possible way to increase the value and pleasure of those hours.

On Monday morning Miss Dulcina Brown, who is Director of the Week-Day Schools of Religion in Portland, Oregon, as well as Director of Religious Education in her own church, led the conference on prayer meetings which train in worship, considering planning and conducting worship services, daily devotions, related memory work, and sources of material. Miss Brown presented a repertoire book, which she invited the workers to add to and draw from.

Tuesday morning was given to a consideration of study and service which train in world friendliness. Miss Mary G. Brown, Public School Supervisor in Corona, California, and active in parent-teacher councils, discussed using the new mission-study materials, growing in the right use of God's gifts, sharing with others, and learning to be Christian citizens. Miss Brown used four illustrated panels upon which she listed the actual service activities in which Junior societies had engaged—for Home Church, Community, Home Mission Fields, and Foreign Missions.

Rev. E. L. Reiner, pastor of the Waveland Avenue Congregational Church, Chicago, presented the important topic of educational evangelism which trains in loyalty to Christ and the church, on Wednesday morning. Personal acceptance of Jesus Christ and vital church membership were discussed practically and helpfully under Mr. Reiner's able leadership.

On the last morning, Mrs. William V. Martin, the talented and efficient superintendent of Illinois, gathered up the discussions of the several days when she outlined building a society program to afford the Juniors practice in Christian living. She took up comprehensive and specific objectives, determining goals, co-operation in accomplishing our task, and illustrated with the Illinois Junior Program and Chart.

In planning for the visiting Junior delegates, the Children's Librarian opened the Children's Room ·and book shelves to them on Monday and arranged for a story-and-game hour to conclude the morning. For Tuesday's treat, the local Junior committee provided cars and took the Juniors on a delightful trip to Golden Gate Park. There was a most interesting period of directed manual activity, presenting Junior committee plans, under the direction of Mrs. Martin, Miss Mary Brown, and Miss Dulcina Brown on Wednesday morning. On Thursday, Mrs. McAfee had planned for these Juniors to participate in the pageant choir.

A Splendid Pageant

Polk Hall and all the corridors were crowded to overflowing on Thursday afternoon when the Juniors of the San Francisco Bay area, under the direction of Mr. Charles Pool, Jr., and Dr. and Mrs. Paul Arnold Peterson for the robed Junior Choir, gave the pageant, "The Junior Crusaders," written by Mrs. Francis E. Clark. Into the pageant, the theme of which is sharing Christ and Christian Endeavor with all children everywhere, Mrs. Clark had written messages received from Christian Endeavorers around the world. At the very climax, when the platform was filled with bright costumes and brighter faces—Japanese children, and Chinese children, and children representing all the nations of the earth—our World President, Dr. Poling, suddenly stood among them to respond to their message of welcome and give them his greeting. As the Juniors wound off the stage in a spiral march and took their seats in front of the platform, Mrs. Clark gave to each a gold ribbon bookmark with the Junior Pledge printed in blue. They then had the special privilege, never-to-be-forgotten, of hearing "Mother Clark's" Message about "Other Juniors." To the pageant committee, Mrs. Ray McAfee, Charles Pool, Jr., Mrs. Charles Pool, Sr., Margaret Verkuyl, and Ella Ware, and to the choir committee, Dr. and Mrs. Paul Arnold Peterson and Gladys Pierce, belong our hearty commendation and grateful appreciation for the success of the pageant and the labor of its preparation.

A "Sailor" Hour

The program for Junior workers included two luncheons. On Monday, the ship motif was used, with large ships centering the tables and small blue-and-white ships marking each place. Mr. Wilbert Martin sounded the Bugle Calls according to U. S. Naval rules— Mess Call, First Call, "Colors," when two small boys in uniform raised the Church Flag, the Christian Endeavor Pennant, and the American Flag to the top of the flag-staff, while all stood at attention with hand over heart, Officers' Call for Mr. Rodeheaver, when he favored us with both instrumental and vocal solos, and again when Dr. Poling arrived to give us "Sailing Orders," and finishing with "Dismiss" and "Secure." A table was occupied by the San Francisco Junior committee, and the chairman, Mrs. McAfee, introduced, in addition to those named above, the following: Florence Fisher, secretary, Ruth Cruse, Mrs. Lawrence Friedline, Mrs. Edouart Bryant, Mary Maclachlan, Jean Balfour, Mrs. L. F. Rodgers, and Mrs. Quandt. Recognition was given and appreciation expressed to this loyal group, whose devotion and sacrificial service made the Junior program possible.

At the Thursday luncheon, the guests were seated about the outside of a hollow square, in the centre of which was a rock garden, built and planted to simulate Mount Rubidoux. The gold cross surmounted its summit and its significance was the better appreciated as Mrs. Poling shared her beautiful experience of the Easter Service at Mount Rubidoux. Rev. Wallace J. Anderson, secretary of the Korean Christian Endeavor Union, just arrived, brought us the appropriate message, "Show Us the Way." Small pots of California poppies at each cover reminded us that this was California's Day. Our gracious hostess for the State, Miss Lorena Burke, presided, and Miss Mary Brown, her successor in the office of State superintendent, sang for us.

One other occasion, the vesper hour with "Mother Clark" on Sunday evening, when she brought a personal message to one hundred and fifty Junior workers on "Some First Things," will never be forgotten by the group who shared in that sacred hour of dedication.

Space does not permit naming those who contributed to the Junior program,—denominational and interdenominational as well as commercial agencies, both local and national, and very many individuals, but I would mention, in addition to the local Junior committee, the most generous assistance of Mr. William Unmack and Miss Grace Fors, and the members of the Junior Staff,—Miss Edna Smith, Secretary, Mrs. William V. Martin and Mr. Wilbert Martin, our artists, who were responsible for decorations, favors, posters, badges, and much more, Miss Mary Brown, Miss Pulcina Brown and Miss Sadie Seaver. To the untiring efforts of these, and to the willing help of the State leaders in attendance upon the convention, we are indebted for what was accomplished.

The Junior staff and Junior leaders would express their deep and enduring gratitude for the inspiration of the presence of "Mother Clark" and Mrs. Poling in our gatherings and for the encouragement given by President Poling, Secretary Sherwood, and Mr. Vandersall.

There were a host of greetings sent to the Junior group, and we owe more than we shall ever know to the prayers of the circle of State superintendents and other friends who joined us daily at His Throne.

THE JUNIOR CRUSADERS

(This pageant, by Mrs. Francis E. Clark, was an inspiring portion of the Thursday afternoon Junior program.)

1. Singing by Junior Choir.
2. Welcome:

> "Friends who come to this convention,
> Come so many miles to meet us,
> From the South and East and Northland,
> Come from many lands to greet us;

> "Friends who come across the border,
> Canada's own sons and daughters;
> Friends who come from other countries,
> Come to us across the waters;

> "We, the California Juniors,
> Gladly welcome you among us;
> Thank you heartily for coming,
> Thank you for the songs you've sung us.

> "You have had your larger meetings,
> Welcomes from the older people;
> You have seen our goodly city,
> Gazed at every spire and steeple;

> "Now we children give you welcome
> To our part of this convention,
> While we tell of our Endeavor,
> Ask you for your kind attention.

> "Hear the words of older people,
> Hear the songs we Juniors sing you;
> Hear the tales of other Juniors,
> And the messages they send you.

> "Quarter of a million children
> Pledged to faithful service ever,
> Send through us their greetings to you,
> To the army of Endeavor."

3. Response
4. Address
5.   PAGEANT: *The Junior Crusaders.*
Recitation:

THE CHILDREN'S CRUSADE

By Margaret J. Preston

Have you read the wonderful story
 Of what happened so long ago,
Away in the Rhenish country,
 In sight of the Alpine snow?

How thousands of little children
 With scallop and staff in hand,
Like Peter the Hermit's pilgrims,
 Set forth for the Holy Land?

From hamlet and town and castle,
  For many and many a day,
These children had seen their fathers
  March to the East away.

"Why do they go?" they questioned
  Of the mothers who watched and wept.
"They go to wrest from the pagan
  The tomb where the dear Lord slept."

And the thought in their young hearts kindled,
  "Let us do as our fathers do;
Let us wear the cross on our shoulder,
  And help in the conquest too.

"The strength of a child is nothing;
  But we'll gather in one strong band
The strength of ten thousand children
  For Christ and the Holy Land."

And, so they tell, these children
  On their strange, wild mission went;
But the Saviour who would not lead them
  In the way He had not sent,

Lifted them up in His pity,
  (Misguided and yet His own)
And, instead of the tomb they sought for,
  Sent them to find His throne.

Now what is the tender lesson
  Wrapped up in the story so,
And what can we learn from the children
  Who perished so long ago?

For the sepulchre's sake where only
  Three days the Redeemer lay,
They were willing to face such peril
  As wasted their lives away.

Are there ten thousand children
  Over this land so broad,
Willing to work, their shoulder
  Wearing the badge of God?

The gifts and the prayers of children,
  Gathered in one strong band,
Could conquer the world for Jesus,
  And make it a Holy Land.

The Choir sings:

        Christ for the world we sing,
        The world to Christ we bring
          With one accord;
        With us the work to share,
        With us reproach to dare.
        With us the cross to bear
          For Christ our Lord.

Recitation by "The Spirit of Christian Endeavor."
> Let us call the roll of the nations,
> > We would know what the children say;
> Let us hear from the young crusaders
> > Who are in the ranks to-day.

The Spirit of Christian Endeavor: "What say the children of *Great Britain* and *America?*"

(Enter children from the *United States* and *Great Britain* and colonies, the choir singing as they march in: tune, "Battle Hymn of the Republic.")

Our eyes behold an army of young soldiers of the Lord,
A quarter of a million strong, His truth their gleaming sword,
In His bright armor panoplied, obedient to His word,
> As they go marching on.

Chorus:
> Glory, glory, glory, hallelujah,
> Glory, glory, glory, hallelujah,
> Glory, glory, glory, hallelujah,
> > They still go marching on.

From all the lands enlisted, East, West, and South and North,
Two hundred fifty thousand, and all of tested worth,
Where'er their Leader calls them they bravely sally forth
> And still go marching on.

Chorus:

Recitation: (One Junior speaking for each country.)
> *Columbia's* happy-faced Juniors
> From the East and the far distant West,
> From the North and the sunny Southland,
> We come at your loving request.

> And we come from distant *Hawaii,*
> And from far-off *Alaska,* too,
> And the children from *Porto Rico*
> Would join the crusade with you.

> From over the *Canada* border
> With songs of glad greeting we come.
> From distant *New Zealand, Tasmania,*
> And our great *Australian* home.

> And the children of dear old *England,*
> Wish to join this crusade with you,
> To conquer the whole world for Jesus,
> To do what He wants us to do.

> From the *Emerald Isle* we greet you,
> From *Wales* and from *Scotland* too,
> Let us join in your glad endeavor,
> We will all be loyal and true.

> We're with you in all your Endeavor;
> We'll join in your prayers and your song;
> For there is but one precious Saviour,
> To whom all the Juniors belong.

The Spirit of Christian Endeavor: "Let us hear from our Southern neighbors."

(Enter children from *Central America, Mexico, South America.*
One child speaks for each.)

As our nearest neighbors we greet you.
From *Central American* lands;
In work for Christian Endeavor
We gladly clasp your hands.

We come from the land where the light and darkness.
The good and the evil are ever at strife;
But *Mexico* too needs Christian Endeavor.
We would find the Way, the Truth and the Life.

Not from the distant Orient, I.
Our land lies 'neath your own fair sky.
Yet *South America,* has need
And earnestly we children plead
That we may join in your crusade,
And, as we can, the work we'll aid.

Recitation by all the children:

From both *Americas* we come.
From *Britain's* empire, too;
Together we'll crusade with Christ,
And strive His work to do.

Singing:

All hail the power of Jesus' name.
Let angels prostrate fall;
Bring forth the royal diadem.
And crown Him Lord of all.

Let every kindred, every tribe
On this terrestrial ball,
To Him all majesty ascribe,
And crown Him Lord of all.

The Spirit of Christian Endeavor: "Let us cross the broad Atlantic, and hear from the children of Europe.'
(Enter one from each land:)

NORTHERN EUROPE: Sweden, Norway, Finland, Latvia, Estonia,
Lithuania, Poland, Denmark.

CENTRAL EUROPE: Germany, Austria, Holland, Switzerland,
Czecho-slovakia, Hungary, Rumania.

SOUTHERN EUROPE: France, Italy, Spain, Greece, Yugo-slavia,
Albania.

All these recite together:

Recitation:

We come from different countries,
With different languages too.
But we're one in Christian Endeavor,
And we gladly join with you.

Spirit of Christian Endeavor: "Let us hear from *Persia* and
Syria. Are you with us in Christian Endeavor?"

(Enter children from *Persia* and *Syria;* one from each country
gives the message:) *Message.*

Spirit of Christian Endeavor: "We would hear from that land which we call the *Holy Land.*"

(Enter two children who recite together:)

Jerusalem is builded as a city that is compact together; whither the tribes go up, the tribes of the Lord. Pray for the peace of Jerusalem.   *Message.*

English-speaking children respond:

And many nations shall come and say, Come; let us go up to the mountain of the Lord, to the house of the God of Jacob, and He will teach us of His ways, and we will walk in His paths; for out of Zion shall go forth the law, and the word of the Lord from Jerusalem.

Spirit of Christian Endeavor: "We would hear from the land of *Egypt.*"

(Enter two children, who recite:)

From the land of the Pharoahs we come,
For we too have Christian Endeavor;
We would join in your earnest crusade,
To make Jesus our King forever.   *Message.*

Spirit of Christian Endeavor: "Let us hear from other children of *Africa.*"

(Enter children, who recite:)

From the Dark Continent we come,
Pleading for help from you,
May we not join in this crusade,
And wear the Red Cross too?
You say you'd win the world for Christ,—
What would He have us do?   *Message.*

Spirit of Christian Endeavor:

What are the children saying,
Away in those Eastern lands,
As they plaintively lift their voices,
And eagerly stretch their hands?
What say the children of *India,* and *Ceylon,* and *Burma?*

(Enter children in costume; they recite:)

Oh, Buddha is cold and distant,
He does not regard our tears;
We've prayed, but he never answers,
We've called, but he never hears.
Yet some of us love the Saviour,
We want to be guided aright;
We are learning through Junior Endeavor,
To walk as children of light.   *Message.*

Spirit of Christian Endeavor: "From the children of *China* we would hear."

(Enter children, who recite:)

From distant homes across the sea,
We come from far Cathay;
In your crusade we'll gladly join,
With you we'll work and pray,
That China's children all may learn
To walk the Jesus way.   *Message.*

Spirit of Christian Endeavor: "Let us hear from *Japan* and *Korea.*"

(Enter children speaking for *Japan and Korea*.)

> We come from the Land of Morning Calm,
> And the Land of the Rising Sun;
> We would join with you in your glad crusade,
> That the Master's will may be done.   *Message.*

Spirit of Christian Endeavor: "Let us hear from the *Islands of the Sea*."

(Enter *Island* children:)

> We bring to you from our island homes
> The children's greeting, "Yok-we-kom."
> In southern seas our islands lie,
> Beneath the burning tropic sky.

> I know God loves both you and me,
> And so He sends across the sea
> His messengers of joy and light,
> To teach us what is pure and right.

> We pray God bless the mission ships,
> And watch them as they sail afar;
> And bless each child whose loving heart
> Holds in God's ship his little part.

English-speaking children respond by singing, (tune, "I Love to Tell the Story.")

> Our mission ships are sailing
> Across the waters blue,
> To tell the sweet old story,
> The Story ever new;
> To carry to the heathen
> So far across the sea,
> The news of that dear Saviour,
> Who died for you and me.

> Spread all the sails, dear children,
> Send the glad news afar,
> Till all the eastern nations
> Shall see once more the star;
> Shall follow where it leadeth
> To find the Lord of light;
> So shall its rays most holy,
> Dispel the shades of night.

Chorus:

> Sailing, the ships are sailing
> Across the waters blue,
> To tell the sweet old story,
> The story ever new.

Spirit of Christian Endeavor: "Are there children here from lands that have no Endeavor?"

(Enter children from Russia, Belgium and Portugal, who recite:)

> No Endeavor in the countries
> Out of which we come to you.
> In your glad crusade for Jesus,
> With your blessed work to do.
> Pray that we may also share;
> We would have Endeavor too.

(Endeavor children of all lands join hands, and form a circle around those with no Endeavor, and sing: "No. 108 in Junior Carols.")

Loyal Juniors, we are striving good Endeavorers to be;
To the battle we are marching, with our banners floating free,
Clad in armor that the Lord provides alike for you and me.

Chorus:

> For Christ we'll win the world,
> Though but children we can fight for right,
> And overcome the wrong;
> We can wear this Christian armor bright,
> And Christ will make us strong.

(Then, still standing in circle, repeat together:)

> The whole wide world for Jesus!
> Once more, before we part,
> Ring out the joyful watchword
> From every grateful heart.

> The whole wide world for Jesus!
> Be this our battle-cry.
> The Crucified shall conquer,
> And victory is nigh.

A marching song, all the children singing:

> Stand up, stand up for Jesus,
> Ye soldiers of the cross.
> Lift high His royal banner,
> It must not suffer loss.
> From vict'ry unto vict'ry
> His army He shall lead,
> Till every foe is vanquished,
> And Christ is Lord indeed.

> Stand up, stand up for Jesus,
> The strife will not be long;
> This day the noise of battle,
> The next the victor's song.
> To him that overcometh
> A crown of life shall be.
> He with the King of glory
> Shall reign eternally.

(At the close of the song, the children march to the front of the platform, and stand in a large circle, holding hands, while the benediction is pronounced.)

CONDENSED MESSAGES USED IN THE
JUNIOR PAGEANT

U. S. POSSESSIONS:

Alaska:

One native Junior Society, the first of its kind; 60 members. The Juniors are doing a big help in our church, bringing each other to church and to the society, and learning to conduct their meetings.

(signed)   Rev. Andrew Wannamaker.

Hawaii:

10 Junior societies; 177 members. We hope some time to have as many Junior as Senior societies.

(signed)   Loi Tsin Chong,
                  Junior Supt. Honolulu Co. C. E. Union.

EUROPE:

Czechoslovakia:

3 Junior societies, 35 members. Our motto from Habakkuk, "I will stand upon my watch." Our purpose, "I will run the way of thy commandments." We pray that each girl would be a little maid of Naaman, telling others about the greatest physician.

(signed)   Gabriela Kallikova.

Finland:

We are only 430; our purpose, to learn to do God's will, and we will try to help the weaker ones.

(signed)   Aina Johanessen.

Germany:

337 Junior societies, with more than 2,000 members. Our purpose, to grow not only in numbers, but also inwardly, that we may better understand and obey the word of God.
(Taken from a number of letters from German boys and girls.)

Great Britain:

1,759 Junior societies, with more than 50,000 members. Our aim, to bring boys and girls to an intelligent and purposeful acceptance of the Junior Christian Endeavor covenant.

(signed)   M. Jennie Street.

Greece:

We are few in number but the spirit of God is with us. We purpose to live for others and serve Him Who came and gave His life a ransom for us.

(signed)   Helen Naase.

Holland:

We have few Juniors but hope to have a larger work. We send this verse, "Jesus called little children unto Him."

(signed)   Yetta Nyland.

Latvia:

10 societies; 80 members. We hope in this year to double our membership and to double our strength and gifts for Jesus.

(signed)   Ch. Freimann.

Norway:

We have 6 Junior societies, with 130 members. We are helping by our singing and by learning Bible texts.

(signed)   Marit,   Gunvor,
                  Hjordis,   Astrid.

Poland:

15 societies, 182 members. We hope to increase our membership and to study and obey God's word. Our verse is, "I love them that love me, and they that seek me early, shall find me."

(signed)   Lydia Kamenz.

Sweden:

4 societies, 40 members. We are trying to lead others to Christ. Our verse is, "I am the Good Shepherd; the Good Shepherd giveth His life for the sheep."

(signed)   Haldis Grondahl.

Constantinople:

1 society, 66 members. We plan to increase our membership, to help each other. We pray that in Christ we may live, and move, and have our being.

(signed)   Ellen W. Catlin.

ASIA:

Burma:
40 societies, 1,000 members. We aim to have Junior Endeavor in every one of our churches in Burma. We try to win children for Christ. Our verse, "I am the light of the world."
(signed)   Ma Than May.

China:
145 societies. We want to help others to know Christ in our villages, our families, our schools, and our churches.
(signed)   S. E. Wong.

India:
We are 121 in number. Our purpose is to grow more like Christ, to help others at all times, remembering that we can do all things through Christ who strengthens us.
(no name signed)

Japan:
We have 23 Junior societies with more than 1,600 members. Junior Christian Endeavor Movement is becoming to a new fashion again in Tokyo from recent year (mainly among the Methodist people). And such meeting is undertaking by youngmens in Yokohama.
(signed)   Masataro Shigematsu.

Korea:
3,000 Juniors of Korea greet you. Our aim to extend the work here by bringing in more members and developing them in a four-fold way as Christ did, in spiritual, mental, physical and social service activities. We also plan to each bring one other Junior to Christ during the year. Our verse, "And Jesus increased in wisdom and stature and in favor with God and man."
(signed)   A Korean Junior.

Syria:
250 Juniors in the Armenian Evangelical churches of Aleppo; also some Intermediate societies for boys.
(signed)   Isabel T. Merrill (Mrs. John E.)

AFRICA:

Egypt:
127 Christian Endeavor societies with 5,474 members. Our purpose is to go forward, fervent in spirit, serving the Lord.
(signed no name)

South Africa, English Union:
14 English-speaking societies, 503 members. We are all servants of Christ. Our purpose is to lead others to Him, because the Son of God loves us and gave Himself for us.
(signed)   Thora McDonald.

AUSTRALIA:

Coo-ee! 26,000 cheerios from Australian Juniors in 950 societies. We are one link in the great Christian Endeavor chain. We are trying to make the link stronger and brighter. We want to be true to Jesus. "The Lord bless thee, and keep thee."
(signed)   Eleanor M. Loader, Junior Supt.

NEW ZEALAND:

100 societies, about 2,500 members, also 5,000 black-skinned brothers and sisters in Samoa. Our purpose is to learn more of Jesus, to love Him more and serve Him better.
(signed)   Frank Charles Clarkson.

From countries with no Junior Endeavor:

ARGENTINA:

> We have a few Christian Endeavor societies but no Juniors
> yet.
>
> (signed)   Mabel Mitchel.

VENEZUELA:

> Several Christian Endeavor societies but no Juniors. We
> are hoping before long we may report Junior work.
>
> (signed)   Maude E. Phillips (Mrs. C. A.)

RUMANIA:

> We have Christian Endeavor societies but no Juniors. We
> are hoping in the future to begin work for them. Our Hun-
> garian name for Christian Endeavor means "straightfor-
> wards" societies.
>
> (signed)   Dr. Arthur Tompa.

SIAM:

> Christian Endeavor, but no Juniors yet in Siam. We plan
> to organize one society very soon. We believe that nothing
> can train our children for Christ quite as well as Junior
> Endeavor.
>
> (signed)   Alice H. Schaefer.

CHRISTIAN ENDEAVOR TOURISTS AT GRAND CANYON

*An entire special train of Christian Endeavorers from the East,
and in addition many other tour parties of delegates in special
cars on regular trains, visited this centre of scenic grandeur
when going to or coming from the International Convention.*

CHAPTER XIV

THE CONVENTION "RESOLVES"

Thanksgiving and Outlook

> *The chairman of the Resolutions Committee, Harry N. Holmes, was assisted by a youth committee representative of State and Provincial Unions of North America. Presidents of such unions chose the young people for this fine service.*

"PRAISE God from Whom all blessings flow!" Christian Endeavororers around the world sing praises to God for the completion of fifty years in the life of the Christian Endeavor movement. From its inspired beginning in the heart and home of the late beloved Francis E. Clark until to-day, Christian Endeavor has been true to its watchword, "For Christ and the Church." It maintains its historic traditions with unbroken loyalty. It calls upon the people of the western world to realize that in Christian Endeavor the Christian church has enrolled its future membership and leadership. With kindred organizations, such as the Epworth League, the Luther League, the Baptist Young People's Union, and similar agencies, it offers its continued services to the church in behalf of the youth of America and the world.

These fifty years enshrine the immortal memory of Dr. Francis E. Clark to whom came "the great ideal, the great idea, and the great name"! We are grateful beyond expression that in the good Providence of God, this convention has the high privilege of the presence of Mrs. Clark to whom we extend our loving and affectionate greetings.

We remember all those leaders who by devotion and challenge guided the early and maturing steps of the movement, and we recall the debt of Christian Endeavor to Dr. John Willis Baer and Dr. James L. Hill, who recently were translated to higher service. The radiant, gifted spirits of these men are still a priceless heritage.

Looking back with gratitude upon fifty golden years, Christian Endeavor resolutely turns its face toward the coming half century and consecrates itself anew to its supreme mission, to make Jesus Christ known to the youth of the world through evangelism, education, and service, and to bring youth into the active service of Christ and the church. Trusting in the Lord Jesus Christ for strength, and upon the leadership of President Daniel A. Poling, it moves forward with steadfast faith and quickened zeal to the end that Christ's Kingdom of righteousness, goodwill, and peace may come on earth as it is in Heaven.

Evangelism, or the World for Christ

The great modern crusade being waged by the Christian Endeavor society is primarily a call to personal consecration to Christ.

Its key-note is evangelism. The appeal to confess sin, to seek forgiveness, to discover the Christ as Saviour and Lord, to dedicate the whole of life to Him,—this is the essence of Christian Endeavor. Therefore, the Christian Endeavorers assembled at the International Convention in San Francisco loyally respond to the challenge to place the highest emphasis upon evangelism during its crusade.

We urge all Christian Endeavor Unions and individual Endeavorers to put forth every effort toward the attainment of the goal of a million young people won for Christ. It is our task to carry the message of Christ to our friends and companions and to all everywhere who do not know Him as their Divine Master. A new surrender of each will to His will and a personal commitment of life are essential. If the religion of Jesus is to conquer the earth, it must be effectively and efficiently taught by each generation of Christians to the succeeding generation. This task is worth the best of our effort, the best of our time, the best of our prayers. We therefore endorse the proposal of a fifty per cent increase in the enrollment of personal workers, a fifty per cent increase in the membership of study classes in the life of Jesus, and a fifty per cent increase in the membership of Comrades of the Quiet Hour.

Christian Endeavor recognizes that the supreme task of the Church is the evangelization of America and the whole world, and, as a part of the church, it dedicates itself to its share of that task. America must be Christianized, first of all, for her own sake. No nation can long exist half Christian and half pagan. America must become Christian or ultimately go the way of all the pagan nations of history. It is Christ or chaos for America. And America must be made Christian for the world's sake. She is either the hope or the despair of the world. She holds in her hand the key to the world's future. No nation is so qualified for the moral and religious leadership of the world as America.

Should our spiritual strength and our religious influence become proportionately as great as our economic power, the evangelization of the world would not be long delayed. To convert selfishness into service, suspicion into faith, discouragement into hope, hatred into love—this is the great problem which confronts the world. There is no adequate way of meeting it other than by the religion of Christian brotherhood and to that task Christian Endeavor is dedicated.

A New Prohibition Slogan

The Christian Endeavor movement, four million strong, confirms its unbroken opposition to the beverage traffic in intoxicating liquors. It rejoices in the adoption of the Eighteenth Amendment to the Constitution of the United States of America and its supporting legislation. It is proud of the part that Christian Endeavor had in bringing prohibition to pass, and pledges its continued loyalty in keeping it in the Constitution and in helping to make it increasingly effective.

The Golden Jubilee Convention of Christian Endeavor goes on record as denouncing the unwarranted attacks that are being made by selfish interests upon the present generation of American youth. Christian Endeavorers regretfully realize that there is still illicit use of beverage alcohol, but know also that present conditions are notably better than those that obtained under the legalized liquor traffic. We call attention to the overwhelming testimony of high-school principals and teachers as to the benefits that have been brought to the schools by the coming of prohibition.

Christian Endeavor, which was born as a crusading movement, gladly hears the call of its leaders to enter upon the present-day crusade to overthrow the illicit traffic in intoxicating liquor. We pledge full support to our president, Daniel A. Poling, and his associates in the Allied Youth movement for the continuance of prohibition. We do not propose to be diverted from our joyously accepted responsibility by false pleas for personal liberty or by the pretence of solicitude for youth at the hands of those who are seeking to bring back a youth-destroying traffic to legalized power.

Christian Endeavor unites with those who thank God because the legalized traffic in intoxicating liquor has gone, and pledge their full measure of loyalty and devotion toward the complete overthrow and removal of the traffic. The slogan adopted by the International Convention of Christian Endeavor in 1911, "A Saloonless Nation by 1920," is enlarged to read, "A nation free from the curse of intoxicating liquor, if it takes fifty more years to bring it to pass."

Christian Endeavor and World-Peace

The Golden Jubilee Convention of Christian Endeavor gladly responds to the call of President Poling to continue the crusade for a world freed from the age-old curse and terror of war. We firmly believe that no generation has possessed such an opportunity to bring nearer fulfilment the prayer of Bethlehem, "Peace on earth, good will to men." We are convinced that nothing more retards the coming of the Kingdom and denies human brotherhood. Christian Endeavor stands for the Peace Pact of Paris and outlawry of armed conflict.

As young citizens of America we urge the Senate of the United States to ratify adherence to the World Court of International Justice. This great agency of world peace has been advocated by the last three Presidents of the United States, and is itself the product of American idealism. The immense moral influence of America must stand behind this great institution at the earliest opportunity. There should be no further delay in our participation.

We rejoice in the leadership of President Hoover, looking forward toward one year's moratorium of intergovernmental debts and reparations. We support with enthusiasm the courageous and sagacious proposal which recognizes the moral and economic unity of the world.

We believe the coming general disarmament conference to be held in Geneva, Switzerland, presents one of the supreme opportunities of our time to further the cause of good will and peace. The Peace Pact abolished war as an instrument of national policy. Sixty nations have signed this treaty. It is now the public law of the world, and it surely implies a drastic reduction in the armed forces of all nations. We urge all Endeavorers to sign the petition to President Hoover distributed at the convention, promising him our unfaltering loyalty as he gives to this great gathering the fullest cooperation.

We sincerely hope that some convinced peace advocates will be included among the American delegation. This conference must succeed. Failure would most certainly be a world calamity.

The Golden Jubilee Convention is for world peace and for all the agencies of the peaceful solution of disputes between nations. We hail the day when there will be a warless world.

On Missions

This convention recognizes that the world cannot live without Christ and we must therefore share Him with others. That was His will and command. We believe and we accept it.

Be it therefore resolved that the Christian Endeavor movement is committed to the missionary task around the world, for this new day demands that we should reach every area of population and every area of life.

As we approach the religions of the world we must go in love and sympathy, recognizing every truth in them so that they will be won to the Christ as the only hope for the world.

Our supreme objective must be to make the world Christian rather than Western. The indigenous church must be given the freedom to accept the fullest responsibility. Christian education must be an outstanding factor in order that the growing educational systems of non-Christian lands shall not become secular and agnostic.

We recognize the culture and power of the non-Christian world and go only in humility, realizing that we and our civilization need Christ as well as they.

We recognize that the task of world missions is just in its genesis. The native churches are just beginning to walk alone. We accept the unparalleled challenge for sacrifice and for life.

The one enemy around the world for the Crusade with Christ is the secular way of life. This permeates our life at home in education, industrialism and every phase of life. Under this philosophy, non-Christian faiths are being dissolved and religion itself is in peril. We therefore commit ourselves, our wealth, our service to the world program of Jesus, that righteousness shall prevail in every area of life and that the world may be saved through Jesus our Lord.

"Remember the Sabbath Day"

The Golden Jubilee Convention affirms its belief in the contribution to human life of the Sabbath Day. Its observance and sanctity is part of the foundation of the structure and concept of America and her institutions. We highly resolve by word and life to preserve the Lord's Day from insidious inroads which threaten this priceless and Divine gift.

We rejoice in the strength of clean bodies.

We have pride in the members of our organization who have achieved distinction on the fields of clean sport.

We welcome to the United States and to California the Olympic Games of 1932. Mindful of the physical, moral, and spiritual well being of all youth and particularly of those Christian Endeavorers who have already been called upon to represent their countries, as well as of those others who may be selected, we respectfully but with utmost earnestness ask that the Olympic Games be closed on Sunday.

Home and Altar

The Golden Jubilee Christian Endeavor Convention states without hesitation a belief that the future depends in large measure upon the Christian home. We believe with all our hearts that the maintenance of the Family Altar is vital to that home. We urge upon every Endeavorer the need of preserving that shrine around which clusters the finest and noblest things of life.

The influence of the home can be undermined by salacious literature, and pictures caricaturing the deepest and holiest things of life. We recommend that a bill be introduced making illegal the stream of filth in pictures, magazines, and books through the postal channels of the United States.

This polluting traffic we condemn, and urge its abolition.

Cigarette Advertising

The International Christian Endeavor Convention strongly condemns the tremendous advertising campaign on billboard and magazine, which tends to fasten habits of cigarette smoking on the boys and girls of America. We deplore this as a menace to the best physical, mental, and spiritual development of youth, and are particularly disturbed at the tendency to break down the high and lofty standards maintained in the past by American womanhood.

THANKS TO ONE AND ALL

The Golden Jubilee Convention of Christian Endeavor is conscious of inadequate words fully to express its gratitude and thankfulness for the welcome, the hospitality, and kindness of its reception in San Francisco. There was surely no other place for the Golden Jubilee but the Golden Gate.

The convention believes that its first duty is to recognize the immeasurable co-operation of the government of the City and County of San Francisco, which assured the success of the convention and the comfort of the delegates, and WHEREAS: Mayor Angelo J. Rossi, the members of the finance committee and of the public welfare committee, who have through their personal efforts and contact, as well as through their position as supervisors of the City and County of San Francisco, been of inestimable service to our convention, and WHEREAS: The entire Board of Supervisors of the City and County of San Francisco has shown its appreciation of the coming of our convention by various acts of official co-operation, now therefore

BE IT RESOLVED: That this Golden Jubilee Convention does hereby extend its very sincere thanks and deep appreciation to the City and County of San Francisco, to its Board of Supervisors, and to all other officials of the city who have been instrumental in their co-operation for the success of this great gathering and

We recognize with thanks the kindness and courtesies received from the chief of police and the members of his department, the San Francisco Convention and Tourist Bureau and its manager, and the exquisite floral Christian Endeavor emblem arranged in Golden Gate Park by the Commissioners and their Superintendent.

The superintendent of the auditorium, and all employees of this beautiful convention hall are remembered in this word of thanks.

It is extraordinarily difficult for the members of this convention to say what is in our hearts about the wonderful work of the Convention Committee. Its machine-like efficiency, never for one single moment losing the touch of kindness and understanding, leaves an indelible impression on the minds of all.

To the Convention Committee of this imperial city, headed by two distinguished citizens, Paul Shoup, general chairman, and Fred D. Parr, associate chairman, we convey the thanks of every guest who has come to the convention. Every desire and every need seem to have been anticipated, and this committee is unsurpassed in all the story of Christian Endeavor conventions. It was worthy of the Jubilee.

William Unmack, the convention secretary, has been a model of stately, kindly, and perfect efficiency.

We wish it were possible to enumerate every member of every committee. This is obviously impossible, but the financing achieved through the untiring efforts of a committee headed by John McGregor and Duncan Matheson, Chairman and Vice-Chairman, merits a special word of recorded praise.

What an inspiration the music and the chorus have been under the leadership of Homer Rodeheaver, his associates, the organist, and the pianists. How we have marvelled at the perfection of the ushering and the devotion of those at the long registration tables. To the chairman and all committeemen who worked so diligently, we offer our thanks.

The convention parade, headed by Colonel Henry G. Matthewson, brought a thrill to all those who participated and to all those who watched.

We know that success would not have crowned the efforts, had it not been for the unstinted and joyful co-operation of the ministers and churches of San Francisco and the Bay Cities, together with the Epworth League and kindred societies. The communion service on Sunday morning was an experience never to be forgotten and would not have been possible but for much thoughtful and careful preparation.

The influence of the convention has been multiplied a thousand fold by the service of the press of the city. By article and illustration, they have carried our message and objective throughout the whole land.

The speakers and conference leaders have placed the convention in great debt by the prophetic and devoted quality of their service.

Especially do we think of Ralph Rambo and Howard Brown, California State Christian Endeavor President and Secretary, respectively, uniting with all Endeavorers of the city and State to make this event overwhelmingly significant.

The convention, in its final session, resolves, while the memory and inspiration are fresh and fragrant, to place on record its sense of abiding gratitude to all who in any way have made the Golden Jubilee Convention such an epoch in the life of Christian Endeavor.

San Francisco and citizens,' the convention will be to all who came, an imperishable memory! You have made religious history in the story of the youth of America.

CHAPTER XV

FELLOWSHIP AND PERSONALITY

A Chapter of Convention Sidelights

A STILL YOUTHFUL SOCIETY

An Editorial on Christian Endeavor in *The San Francisco Chronicle*

Five million or what multiple of five million? Who can tell how many earnest young souls are represented by the delegates now gathering for the International Convention of Christian Endeavor at San Francisco? The most careful statistics must necessarily fall short of the fact. Society enrolment tells only part of the story. Beyond the membership ranks are other multitudes, enrolled in other societies, which first derived their inspiration from the Christian Endeavor movement.

Even if these were all counted, the roster would still be incomplete. For behind these shock troops is a great unorganized army, a multitude whose lives have been, knowingly or unaware, influenced by the Endeavorers. And then there is that other great army of veterans, men and women, now not actively connected with a Christian Endeavor organization, but upon whose character the society put an indelible stamp in their younger days.

Half a century ago at Portland, Me., Rev. Francis E. Clark gathered fifty boys and girls in the parlor of his parsonage, and pledged them to the principles and discipline that still remain the basis of the Christian Endeavor and other church societies modelled on its lines. That there was something enduring and vital in those principles admits of no debate. The phenomenal growth of Christian Endeavor is stubborn historical evidence to confound sceptics. The tenacity with which the Endeavor movement holds its own in this later era of new standards or no standards is evidence of durability.

Fifty years after its founding Christian Endeavor is still a young people's society. Youth is its field, the source of supply for its raw material. The Endeavorers, for all their deference to veteran leadership, are still inspired by the enthusiasm of youth . . . San Francisco is honored to be the host of the Golden Jubilee Convention of Christian Endeavor.

LUNCHEONS AND DINNERS

The Friday, July 10, dinner in honor of speakers and officers of the convention is reported in Chapter I of this book. This was a delightful affair with short talks that scintillated with wit and humor.

A fellowship dinner at 5.30 o'clock on July 11, opening day of the convention, "broke the ice" in the convention's fellowship activities. Delegates went from this event to the first evening session, at which the keynote address was given. Clarence C. Hamilton, publication-manager of the International Society, presided at this enjoyable banquet.

Christian Vocations Luncheon

On Sunday noon, July 11, a capacity crowd of three hundred young people thronged the banquet hall of the Clinton Cafeteria, to consider together the problems of vocational choice. Stanley B. Vandersall, of the International Society, was in charge of the program. Spirited singing of gospel songs was followed by the introduction of the two guest speakers, Harry N. Holmes, president of the New York State Christian Endeavor Union, and Dr. C. Y. Cheng, executive secretary of the National Christian Council of China.

Mr. Holmes centred his remarks around four progressive declarations for the individual—namely, I am, I can, I ought, I will. Dr. Cheng described briefly the need for Christian workers in China.

As is customary in California State Union conventions, the superintendent of Life Work in the State union, Mrs. Howard L. Brown, announced the names of a score of Life-Work Recruits who had completed the first, second, or third year of the program of work outlined by this department. Mr. Vandersall presented appropriate certificates of recognition.

Tuesday's Banquets

Many Junior workers joined for a splendid luncheon, with Dr. Daniel A. Poling as speaker and Miss Mildreth Haggard as chairman.

A dinner for trustees of the International Society, field secretaries, State presidents, and International Society officers was held Tuesday.

Vice-president Foulkes was chairman.

The Intermediate banquet, held at the West Side Christian Church, San Francisco, as a feature of the convention, was open to all Intermediates, all high-school students, and all young people under nineteen years of age.

Many more than four hundred attended.

The arrangements were in charge of Benjamin A. March, Intermediate chairman for the San Francisco local committee. The splendid meal was served by the ladies of the West Side Church, and at an expense of only forty cents a plate. Songs, yells, and pep marked the occasion. The Hawaiians and many other delegations gave "specials." State Intermediate superintendents were introduced. The convention accordionist, Rev. A. J. Ungersma of Waterville, Wash., gave several numbers, and also helped in the general fellowship of the occasion.

Luncheons for Pastors

Two well-attended luncheons for pastors were held, one on Wednesday where Dr. Poling presided, and one on Thursday, with Harry N. Holmes in charge.

College Students Meet

Two well-attended and beneficial luncheons for college students were held on the last two days of the convention, in the Whitcomb Hotel. The attendance each day was seventy-five, and no fewer than thirty colleges were represented each day, from New England and Florida to Washington State and California.

The program in each instance was in charge of Stanley B. Vandersall, Christian Vocations superintendent of the International Society. Special music was a feature. Rev. Wallace J. Anderson, Seoul, Korea, and Rev. Harry Thomas Stock, D. D., of the Congregational Education Society were the speakers.

The students attending expressed a desire for a more detailed series of conferences on college work and Christian Endeavor in the next International convention.

Alumni Banquet

The largest fellowship dinner of the convention was given by alumni and younger members to the number of 700 in honor of Mrs. Francis E. Clark. The program of this memorable occasion is given in Chapter IX.

NUGGETS OF THE GOLDEN STATE

The Higgins Sisters, four girls from Shenandoah College, Virginia, sang on several occasions during the convention. Theirs is the crooning style of vocalism, and all the voices are pleasing. The sisters, Sally, Ida Maye, Alice, and Katherine, wore identical costumes when appearing on the platform. In the Dixie section of the parade they appeared in Asiatic costumes, and held streamers attached to a float which represented the spread of the gospel.

Five Junior girls from Utah sang several hymns at the convention-faculty breakfast on the fifth day of the convention. One contralto voice held its own against the four soprano singers.

Caroline Hilliard, San Rafael, Cal., won the convention poster contest. Emmy Lou Osborne, Seattle, Wash., and George H. Blaine, Jr., New York N. Y., were awarded second and third prizes, respectively. The award was made on the basis of advertising appeal, coloring, and Christian Endeavor spirit.

Dr. J. Whitcomb Brougher, pastor of Tremont Temple, Boston, and a former Californian, was to have spoken twice in the International Christian Endeavor Convention. He was heard at the pre-convention banquet of July 10, and some of those present remarked a huskiness in his voice, which usually rings with silver tones. But all were shocked to learn a few hours later that Dr. Brougher was confined to the home of a friend in Oakland threatened with an attack of pneumonia. Dr. Brougher made a speedy recovery, but to the disappointment of the delegates was unable to speak in the convention sessions.

What a whoop from Clifford Earle's Wisconsin Christian Endeavor boosters came with the announcement that Milwaukee had been selected as the 1933 International Convention city! A warm welcome awaits North American youth in this growing city of the Mid-West, a city that has shown real progress in religion, education, and industry. Indianapolis was among the several cities that, while enthusiastically claiming the convention, good-naturedly consented that 1933 be Milwaukee's year to entertain' this most significant of young people's conventions of any nature.

Booths with interesting exhibits lined the spacious corridors of the auditorium. The various States had their own booths, and, of course, the various departments of Christian Endeavor work, like Junior, Intermediate, missionary, and so forth. The posters showed careful thought and preparation, and the handwork was decidedly helpful in showing what young people can do. The Presbyterian U. S. A. booth had machines showing not only stereopticon but also moving pictures, which give a fine idea of missionary work. Just to visit the booths and note the information given in them was enough to give material for a helpful report of the convention.

In the Intermediate exhibit at the convention a particularly interesting feature was the series of model meeting-rooms constructed by California members on a miniature scale. One could wish that several of these rooms might actually be reproduced in a full-sized room, so attractive and well planned were these models.

A roll-call of nations, conducted in the International Christian Endeavor Convention on July 14, showed that in addition to the North American delegates from the United States, Canada, and Mexico there were Christian Endeavorers present from Persia, China, Japan, Siam, Alaska, Finland, England, Scotland, Wales, Ireland, New Zealand, Denmark, Colombia (South America), Germany, Korea, and Australia. Missionaries of ten denominations were in attendance.

In between the big, dominating things of the convention, there bubbled up delightful little asides, in which hearts throbbed generously with whole-souled neighborliness.   For instance, there was that Guardian Angel who hovered so protectingly over the precious little lady whom all called Mother Clark. Mrs. Daniel A. Poling came across the continent with the wife of the founder and first chief of Christian Endeavor at her side.

But everyone wanted to "protect" Mother Clark from the bustling crowds of the convention! "Please stand aside; you are in front of Mother Clark," some young person would thoughtfully remind us, as a line of committees or field secretaries formed on the platform for introductions.

How the brief messages of this beloved companion of Francis E. Clark did please and thrill sympathetic hearers! The clear ringing tones and the ever-smiling face will always remain in memory.

A burly Irish policeman stopped at a street crossing near the Exposition Auditorium to smile in a fatherly way at a midget Italian newsboy, tousle-headed and with a rather pinched expression. "Sellin' the goods?" asked the policeman "Only three," answered the boy. "Brace up; you'll sell a lot more."

The conversation was overheard by a keen-faced man with the convention badge, one of a group. "Give me six," he called to the boy. Then he turned to his companions. "You'll want papers to send home," he said, "Come and buy some." And the boy's stock in trade dwindled, while his face shone.

A little woman drew a four-year-old boy in a child's express wagon along McAllister Street, through the Civic Centre, and up and down near the auditorium.   Her wan, drawn face caught the eye of one of the Christian Endeavor girls, who sensed the woman's suspense and weariness. "Come inside and enjoy the singing," she suggested to the woman. "I'll stay with the little boy. We don't mind missing a little out of so very much." And the woman smilingly went into the hall.

WHO'S WHO ON THE PROGRAM

The following are in addition to speakers listed elsewhere as officers of the International Society of Christian Endeavor, trustees, field secretaries, and members of the Executive Committee:

Rev. O. T. Anderson, St. Louis, Mo., Editor, "Front Rank."
Rev. Wallace J. Anderson, Secretary, Korean Christian Endeavor Union.
Mary Babcock, Occidental College, Los Angeles.
Rev. Jesse M. Bader, D. D., Indianapolis, Secretary of Evangelism, United Christian Missionary Society.

Mrs. Catherine Miller Balm, Philadelphia, Director, Young People's Work, Reformed Church, United States.

Ethel Boxell, Minneapolis, Minn., President, Minnesota Christian Endeavor Union.

Rev. J. Whitcomb Brougher, D. D., Pastor, Tremont Temple, Boston, Mass.

Rev. Aaron Brown, Pensacola, Florida, Young People's Department, A. M. E. Zion Church.

Mrs. Howard L. Brown, Los Angeles, Calif., Life Work Recruit Superintendent, California Christian Endeavor Union.

Rev. Lloyd R. Carrick, St. John's Presbyterian Church, San Francisco, Calif.

C. Y. Cheng, LL. D., Shanghai, China, Moderator of the United Church of Christ in China.

Mrs. Francis E. Clark, Boston, Mass., Mother of Christian Endeavor.

Dr. A. E. Cory, Indianapolis, Indiana, Director, National Pension Fund, Disciples of Christ.

Bert H. Davis, Utica, N. Y., Author, "Leadership Through Christian Endeavor."

Rev. Louis H. Evans, Pastor, First Presbyterian Church, Pomona, Calif.

Rev. Fred B. Fisher, D. D., Ann Arbor, Mich., former Methodist Missionary Bishop of India.

Rev. W. Arnett Gamble, Raymond, Miss., President, Mississippi Christian Endeavor Union.

Rev. Frank D. Getty, Philadelphia, Pa., Director, Young People's Work, Presbyterian Church, U. S. A.

Bishop J. A. Gregg, Nashville, Tenn., A. M. E. Church.

Mildreth J. Haggard, Minneapolis, Junior Representative, International Society of Christian Endeavor.

Verna Harvey, President, Arizona Christian Endeavor Union.

James Henderson, Portland, Oregon, President, Oregon Christian Endeavor Union.

Rev. Louis B. Hillis, D. D., Berkeley, Calif., Pastoral Counsellor.

Harry N. Holmes, New York, Secretary, World Alliance for International Friendship Through the Churches; President, New York State Christian Endeavor Union.

J. Gordon Howard, Dayton, Ohio, National Director, Young People's Work, Presbyterian Church, U. S. A

Earl Israel, Allentown, Pa., President, Pennsylvania Christian Endeavor Union.

Mary E. Jackson, President, West Virginia Christian Endeavor Union.

Rev. William States Jacobs, D. D., First Presbyterian Church, Houston, Texas.

Nettie Kilgore, Hot Springs, Ark., President, Arkansas Christian Endeavor Union.

Lily King, Salt Lake City, President, Utah Christian Endeavor Union.

Rev. Herman A. Klahr, Associate Pastor, Old Stone Presbyterian Church, Cleveland, Ohio.

Bishop L. Westinghouse Kyles, Winston-Salem, N. C., A. M. E. Zion Church.

C. Fayette Lawrence, Katonah, N. Y., Trustee, New York State Christian Endeavor Union.

Rev. Lawrence C. Little, D. D., National Director, Young People's Work, Methodist Protestant Church.

Edmund L. Lucas, Ph.D., D. D., President, Forman Christian College, Lahore, India.

Rev. W. A. MacTaggart, D. D., Toronto, Canada, President, Toronto Conference, United Church of Canada; Hon. President, Canadian Christian Endeavor Union.

H. Lewis Mathewson, San Francisco, Vice-President, California Christian Endeavor Union.

Rev. Mark A. Matthews, D. D., Pastor, First Presbyterian Church, Seattle, Wash. (This church has 33 Christian Endeavor Societies.)

Rev. Lapsley A. McAfee, D. D., Pastor Emeritus, First Presbyterian Church, Berkeley, California.

Rev. Lawrance J. Mitchell, San Francisco, Official Organist.

Rev. S. S. Morris, Nashville, Tenn., A. M. E. Zion Church.

Otto Nielson, Fort Worth, Texas.

Fred D. Parr, San Francisco, Associate Chairman, Convention Committee.

Paul Pitman, Director, Radio Station KPO, San Francisco.

Rev. Charles C. Poling, Salem, Oregon.

Rev. E. W. Praetorius, D. D., Cleveland, Ohio, National Director, Young People's Work, Evangelical Church.

Ralph Rambo, Los Angeles, President, California Christian Endeavor Union.

Mrs. Margaret Weaver Reid, Contralto, New York.

Rev. E. L. Reiner, Waveland Avenue Congregational Church, Chicago.

Homer Rodeheaver, Director of Music, New York.

Col. Raymond Robins, Chicago, former National Chairman, Progressive Party; former American Red Cross Commissioner to Russia.

Hon. James Rolph, Jr., Sacramento, Governor of California.

Robert Ropp, Ohio, President of "Allied Youth."

Hon. Angelo J. Rossi, Mayor of San Francisco.

Rev. George H. Scofield, D. D., Ph.D., First Presbyterian Church, Walla Walla, Wash.

Rev. Herbert P. Shaw, D. D., West Side Christian Church, San Francisco.

Moses M. Shaw, Chicago, National Director, Young People's Work, United Presbyterian Church.

William Shaw, LL. D., Santa Monica, Calif., former General Secretary of the International Society of Christian Endeavor.

Paul Shoup, San Francisco, General Chairman, Convention Committee.

Rev. Harry Thomas Stock, D. D., Boston, National Secretary, Young People's Work, Congregational Church.

T. T. Swearingen, Indianapolis, Associate Director, Young People's Work, United Christian Missionary Society.

Rev. Morris H. Turk, D. D., Pastor, Williston Congregational Church, Portland, Maine.

William Unmack, San Francisco, Convention Committee Director.

Rev. Walter W. Van Kirk, New York, Associate Secretary, Federal Council of Churches of Christ in America.

Rev. Ezra Allen Van Nuys, D. D., Calvary Presbyterian Church, San Francisco.

James S. Webster, Associate Chairman, 1897 San Francisco, International Christian Endeavor Convention Committee.

Lenadell Wiggins, Pennsylvania, Field Secretary, National W. C. T. U.

Hon. Curtis D. Wilbur, San Francisco, U. S. Circuit Justice, former Secretary of the Navy.

Hattie Mae Wood, Amarillo, Texas, President, Texas Christian Endeavor Union.

www.ingramcontent.com/pod-product-compliance
Lightning Source LLC
Chambersburg PA
CBHW020949030426
42339CB00004B/15